# The Wounded Heart of THOMAS MERTON

Robert Waldron

PAULIST PRESS
New York/Mahwah, NJ

Cover photo by Jim Forest
Cover design by Sharyn Banks
Book design by Lynn Else

Library of Congress Cataloging-in-Publication Data

Waldron, Robert G.
    The wounded heart of Thomas Merton / Robert Waldron.
        p. cm.
    Includes bibliographical references.
    ISBN 978-0-8091-4684-0 (alk. paper)
    1. Merton, Thomas, 1915–1968—Psychology. 2. Jungian psychology—Religious aspects—Catholic Church. 3. Depression, Mental—Religious aspects—Catholic Church. 4. Merton, Thomas, 1915–1968. I. Title.
    BX4705.M542W36 2011
    271′.12502—dc22
    [B]

                                                                    2010050638

Published by Paulist Press
997 Macarthur Boulevard
Mahwah, New Jersey 07430

www.paulistpress.com

Printed and bound in the
United States of America

*Dedicated to*
*Margaret C. Waldron and Julia Flynn Renna*

I am not physically tired, merely filled with a deep, undefined vague sense of spiritual distress as if I had a deep wound running, inside me, and it had to be stanched.

—Thomas Merton, *Run to the Mountain:*
*The Journals of Thomas Merton,*
*Volume 1, 1939–1941,* 452

# Contents

# Preface

*The Wounded Heart of Thomas Merton* is a Jungian interpretation of the life and the work of Trappist monk Thomas Merton. I consider myself qualified to write such a book because I have studied Jungian theory most of my adult life. As far as Thomas Merton is concerned, I have been reading and studying him ever since I read his autobiography, *The Seven Storey Mountain*, during my junior year in high school in the early 1960s.

I do not claim or pretend to be a psychiatrist, psychologist, or therapist. I admire the man Thomas Merton and his writings, and in my attempts to understand him more as a man, a monk, a priest, and an artist, I have found that Carl Jung's theory of individuation has, over the years, shed much light on Merton and his work, allowing me to understand more fully the origin, the vicissitudes, and the hard-won insights of his spiritual journey. Thus, let me announce loudly and clearly that I am offering readers my interpretation of Merton's life and work, employing Jungian theory as my guidepost and paradigm.

As with all interpretation, whether it is a biography of a life, or an exegesis of a poem, novel, play, symphony, or painting, no one has to *accept* the interpretation. One may agree with certain portions of the interpretation and disagree with others, or one can reject the complete interpretation. It is ultimately the concern of the reader and not the author. My only hope is that I will indeed shed some light on Thomas Merton, a very complicated man who deserves the efforts of attentive, close reading. I do not, however, claim to have plumbed the mystery of Merton, for every person is an enigma, but I have, after years of reading and studying his life, won for myself what I believe is a deeper, more whole understanding of his life and his goals as a Religious and as an artist, and I want to share the insights I have gained with others who are also interested in Thomas Merton.

To be candid, I believe that Thomas Merton represents for our time the spiritual seeker par excellence or rather, to borrow Carl Jung's phrase, he is our best Christian (Catholic, if you will) example of a "modern man in search of a soul." And the most alluring aspect of Merton's seeking is that he indeed found his soul, thus offering hope to millions of people who today have embarked on their own search for meaning in their lives.

*The Wounded Heart of Thomas Merton* can also serve as a well-rounded, sympathetic introduction to Thomas Merton for those who are new to his life, his writing, and, yes, his message.

# Acknowledgments

Portions of *The Wounded Heart of Thomas Merton* first appeared in my book, *Thomas Merton in Search of His Soul: A Jungian Perspective*. Having been composed before the publication of Merton's unexpurgated journals, those portions have been updated and amplified.

To Sandra Walter for her superb editing and encouragement. To Paul Pearson, the director and archivist of the Merton Center in Kentucky for his kindness and helpfulness. To the editor of *The Merton Seasonal*, Patrick O'Donnell, for sharing his essay "*Sunken Islands: Two and One-Fifth Unpublished Merton Poems* (*The Merton Seasonal*, spring, 1987).

"Elias—Variations on a Theme," "The Anatomy of Melancholy," and "Whether There Is Enjoyment in Bitterness," by Thomas Merton, from THE COLLECTED POEMS OF THOMAS MERTON, copyright © 1957 by The Abbey of Gethsemani. Reprinted by permission of New Directions Publishing Corp.

"Hagia Sophia," by Thomas Merton, from THE COLLECTED POEMS OF THOMAS MERTON, copyright © 1963 by The Abbey of Gethsemani. Reprinted by permission of New Directions Publishing Corp.

I would like to thank the former publisher of Paulist Press, the late Rev. Lawrence Boadt, CSP; my editor, Kevin di Camillo; and my friend Brother Patrick Hart, OCSO, for their help and encouragement in the writing of this book.

# Introduction

Although much has been written about Thomas Merton since his tragic death in 1968, few scholars have focused at length on his life-long battle with depression. In *The Wounded Heart of Thomas Merton*, I will address Merton's depression, which commenced with his mother's death from cancer when he was six years old. It intensified with the death of his father from brain cancer when Merton was a teenager, and it remained an ongoing problem throughout his adolescence and adulthood. As a young man, Merton was tempted to commit suicide on at least two occasions, and during his time as a monk in the monastery, he refers in his journals to three nervous breakdowns.

His depression is one of the reasons his years as a student at Cambridge University were such wild, Augustinian days fraught with too much partying and chasing girls, its tragic outcome his fathering of a child. He was an unhappy, neurotic young man; to borrow Carl Jung's phrase, he was a "modern man in search of a soul." He would indeed find his soul, but not until after much suffering and soul-searching.

After the scandal of Merton's fathering a child, his guardian, Tom Bennett, suggested that Merton leave England to begin anew in America. Merton was happy to be granted another chance, to travel to a new place to change his life around. But as a student at Columbia University, he fell into the same old habits, and as his disgust with himself grew, he suffered from deeper bouts of depression.

At times he felt that his life was meaningless. Being a voracious reader, he sought answers to his many questions about life in books; he also longed to be a published author, in particular, a novelist. Writing failed to offer him the peace he so desperately needed, however, and he finally turned to religion for answers, finding them in Catholicism. He was baptized a Catholic in 1938; he continued to write, but his career as a writer had not taken off as he had hoped. Publishers were not interested in his novels, and literary journals were not interested in his poems; the *New Yorker* rejected many of his poems.

As a Catholic, he began to feel he had a vocation to the Religious life. He applied to the Franciscan order and was tentatively accepted. But after admitting that he had fathered a child in England, the order rescinded its admittance. Merton was devastated. On a suggestion from his friend, philosophy teacher Dan Walsh, Merton went on retreat at the Trappist Abbey of Gethsemani in Kentucky. He fell in love with the place and its way of life. He applied for acceptance and was quickly admitted as a novice.

Many people believe that after his conversion to Catholicism and subsequent entry into the Abbey of Gethsemani, Merton had finally and forever found the "peace that passeth understanding," but as we shall see, Merton the monk struggled with a number of issues, including depression. He was not, however, so debilitated that he could not write. He went on to become one of America's best-selling spiritual writers, his success launched by his autobiography *The Seven Storey Mountain*, now considered a classic, to be followed by such books as *Seeds of Contemplation, The Sign of Jonas*, and *No Man Is an Island*. Including his posthumous work, Merton wrote over sixty books.

His autobiography serves as one of the best modern confessions of a depressive ever written, eloquently chronicling his search for depression's antidote: peace of mind and soul. People who have read and admired Merton's books on spirituality often find it paradoxical that a man referred to as a "spiritual master" (Lawrence S. Cunningham's description of Merton) would be subject to depression, but the fact is that many highly gifted men and women suffer from depression.

Many readers will wonder if he sought psychological therapy. He did, but it did not help him much. He intuitively understood James Hillman's idea that depression is hidden knowledge, and if one listens carefully to the still, small voice, one will be shown how to achieve wholeness (*holiness*, if you will), and Merton followed his inner self's wisdom. Similar to that of another depressive, William Styron, author of the best-selling book on depression, *Darkness Visible*, Merton discovered that inner healing lay waiting for him in silence and solitude: Styron writes, "For me, the real healers were peace and seclusion." Merton followed a similar path.

A book such as *The Wounded Heart of Thomas Merton* may trouble some readers, particularly those unaware of Merton's psychological struggles; it may disturb them in the same fashion that Mother Teresa's recently published papers have shocked Catholics over the world, revealing, as they clearly do, that she suffered not only from depression for much of her adult life, but abided in a dark night of the soul for decades. But holy men and women are not immune to depression; it is nothing to be ashamed about no matter what one's station is in life. It can and does happen to anyone.

Depression, however, *still* carries a stigma, but in Merton's day it was much worse: He often felt ashamed of himself. For much of his young life, he also suffered from a guilt complex; as a young man, he sought relief from it in reckless (and what he considered sinful) behavior, like excessive drinking and sexual promiscuity. As we shall see, he brought his guilt along with him into the monastery.

Considering his life as a whole, we shall see that it illustrates the biblical wisdom that where sin abides, grace abounds. Like his beloved Dante, he had been lost in a dark wood, but he found the golden string of Catholicism, which led him out of his confusion and despair and away from suicide. In short, if circuitously, it led him to God.

In most monasteries today, it should be mentioned, a master of admissions would perhaps not accept Merton as a monastic candidate, instead recommending that he seek psychological therapy. We can be grateful that the Trappists were not as strict in their admission's policy as they are today, candidates now having to pass a number of psychological tests and intensive interviews before they are admitted as postulants. Otherwise, the spiritual master we know and love as Thomas Merton, who has inspired millions of readers, would never have emerged from the kiln of Western monasticism, a way of life still available to spiritual sojourners of the twenty-first century.

Merton's entry into the Abbey of Gethsemani is reminiscent of Martin Luther's becoming a monk. Erik Erikson writes:

> This new life, however, was one which made an institution out of the very configuration of being walled in. Architecturally, ceremonially, and in its total world-mood, it symbolized life on this earth as a self-imposed and self-conscious prison with only one exit, and that one to eternity. The acceptance of this new frame of life had made him, for a while, peaceful and "godly"; at the same time of his fit, however, the sadness was deepening again.[1]

We shall follow Merton's journey and see that he begins, like Luther, to be quite happy in the beginning of his monastic life, but depression lurks in the background ever ready to pounce upon the young man. It does so on many occasions, as it had on the fourteenth anniversary of his priesthood when he writes this astonishing assessment of his life: "I wish I could say they had been fourteen years of ever-growing fulfillment and order and integration...but now I realize more and more the depth of my frustration and the apparent finality· of my defeat...as if in a way my priestly life has been sad and fruitless—the defeat and failure of my monastic life."[2]

His depressions, however, yielded more and more self-knowledge, more knowledge about his shadow, and this led to greater individuation, thus a greater wholeness of personality. Notice I do not say "perfection," which was Merton's initial goal (to become a saint as suggested to him by his best friend Robert Lax), but *wholeness*, which Jung defines:

> Wholeness is to be equated with health. As such, it is both a potential and a capacity. We are born possessing fundamental wholeness but, as we grow, this breaks down and reforms into something more differentiated. Expressed in this way, the achievement of conscious wholeness may be regarded as the goal or purpose of life. Interaction with others or the environment may or may not facilitate this, as the case may be.[3]

When he turns fifty years old, he understands the wisdom of becoming a monk:

> The monastery is a school—a school in which we learn from God how to be happy...What has to be healed in us is our true nature, made in the likeness of God. What we have to learn is love. The healing and the learning are the same thing.[4]

In conclusion, the purpose of *The Wounded Heart of Thomas Merton* is to examine the extent to which Merton faced his depression and to what degree he achieved psychological and spiritual wholeness, which in essence means to what extent he found healing for his heart, wounded at the tender age of six.

# Chapter One

"Start at the beginning" a child will invariably beg a parent who is about to read a favorite bedtime story for the thousandth time. Children are like that, no shortcuts, no compromises when it comes to storytelling. It is also wise advice for the biographer to start at the beginning, for I believe in the Wordsworthian wisdom that "the child is father of the man."[1]

To understand the *man* Thomas Merton, we must begin with his relationship with his mother. She was surely a loving mother, desiring only the best for her first child. She also had definite ideas about raising her child, and rather than follow her motherly instinct, she relied on a book of child rearing. Thus, at an early age, the child Merton became joined at the hip to his mother, along with her book. There was another book too, a diary Merton's mother kept, noting her son's progress as he grew physically, psychologically, and intellectually. In his autobiography *The Seven Storey Mountain*, Merton admits that on reading the diary, he discovered that he was no mother's "dreamchild," that he was a difficult child, stubborn, and unpredictable— which is probably true of most children![2]

What astonishes readers today is the *scientific* way his mother chose to raise her child. It suggests coldness and calculation about her approach to nurturing. It is sad to read that Merton regarded his mother as a distant, severe figure and stinting in her expression of love; it surely had a negative effect on his future relationships with women. The pivotal experience in Merton's childhood is his mother's death from stomach cancer. It is heartbreaking to read about six-year-old Merton being driven with his family in a rented car to the hospital to visit his dying mother. The boy Thomas, however, was not allowed out of the car to join the family in their last visitation. With the driver, he remained in the rain-streaked car, awaiting the return of his father and family. His father had previously given his son a hand-written note from his mother. He took the note out to the back-yard where, under a maple tree, he read it. It took him a while finally to understand its import: His mother was dying, and he would never see her again.

Here in its raw tragedy, we see the first, serious wounding of Merton's heart. It is such a profound experience that Carl Jung would describe it as archetypal in its significance. It is an Edenic story, of Adam's being expelled from Eden, for Merton's child-hood is now over, his Eden gates shut forever. Remembering the event in his mid-twenties, he described it, "And a tremendous weight of sadness and *depression* settled on me. It was not the grief of a child, with pangs of sorrow and many tears. It had something of the heavy perplexity and gloom of adult grief. And was therefore all more of a burden because it was to that extent, unnatural"[3] [emphasis added].

In his description of his mother's death, the word *depression* leaps from the page. Depression descended upon the boy at a young age, and it would reappear many times throughout his life. One might even wonder if he had become a melancholic at the moment of his mother's death. Most people who knew Merton well would likely say he did *not* possess such a temperament, that he was a spontaneous, fun-loving, extroverted, people-loving person. After closely reading his journals, however, one sees that melancholy (depression) became his constant companion, one he learned to coexist with—but more of that later.

Merton's reading his note under the maple tree is reminis-cent of the tree of knowledge in the Garden of Eden. He was at first confused, until finally its significance dawned on him. For a six-year-old to understand death is as difficult as for us to understand God; St. Augustine says it is like a child trying to transfer the ocean into his beach hole.[4] But one thing is certain: His mother would no longer be part of his life.

With his mother absent, so is absent the feminine and all that the feminine implies: physical security, affection, human touch, attention, emotional security, and motherly nurturing, even though hers was stinting. If we keep in mind the boy holding the note in his hand, we can perhaps understand why the written word later became so important to Merton, why as a teenager he informed his Aunt Maud he wanted to be a writer.[5] We also understand why he became a voracious reader, as words contained life-important information, even words that spoke of life's greatest pain and mystery: death. Words were also Merton's last link with his mother, she who kept a diary of her son's childhood growth and behavior; it is not a great leap for us to understand why he became one of the last century's great diarists, as prolific and important as Julian Green, Virginia Woolf, Anaïs Nin and André Gide.

In summary, the archetypal imagery of Adam and Eve and the tree of knowledge and of the expulsion from the Garden of Eden helps us to understand that we can never underestimate the utter importance of that fateful day when Merton struggled to understand his mother's last written words to her son. We might question the wisdom of her manner of informing her son of her imminent death. Was it coldhearted? She was more likely sparing her son the pain of seeing her die, but she may have left behind a psychologically healthier son had she allowed him into the hospital room for a last good-bye and embrace.

When the family members left the hospital, they quickly drove home to Douglaston, on New York's Long Island. Merton followed his father up the stairs to the bedroom. From the threshold of his father's room, the boy watched his father weep at the window. This sight must have been harrowing for Merton to witness. But what about the boy himself? Why was there not someone caring for him, nurturing him in his grief? He had lost his mother, and he too was grieving, but there is no indication in Merton's account of the day of his mother's death of anyone attending to *him*, which must have been a festering wounding of his heart and head. He was essentially alone. Had loneliness that day accosted him forever? Had he, on an existential level, intuitively understood that we are all essentially alone? Is it possible that for the rest of his life he had difficulty forming lasting relationships with the opposite sex because of this loneliness, due to the "abandonment" of his mother's dying? Is his mother's death somehow related to what he later admits to as his "refusal of woman"? (These questions are to be explored later.)

This pattern of being alone would dominate his life—even to his taking vacations to Europe alone, never with a friend, neither male nor female. (Later in life, as a monk, he does fall in love with his nurse called M. in hospital, but more of this later.)

There followed a subsequent journey in a rented car, transporting the family to the crematorium. Merton remained alone in the car, relieved not to have seen the coffin glide beyond the pane into the furnace, a horrific image for a young child to be left with for the rest of his life. Yet, imagining it is perhaps just as horrific.

Carl Jung states that we are psychologically androgynous; a man's feminine component is called the *anima* and a woman's masculine component is called the *animus*. Psychological growth for both a man and a woman demands the integration of the contra-sexual archetype. The specific function of a man's anima is to serve as a mediatrix between the ego, the center of consciousness, and the Self, the center of the unconscious mind, which also serves as the regulating force of the whole psyche.

When a man listens to his anima, he is led into the deepest regions of the unconscious mind where the sources of wisdom and self-knowledge lie. The anima also assists a man in discovering the personal symbols that will release Eros, the principle of relatedness without which he cannot connect with the Self or with people in the external world. The anima likewise provides the Eros (energy) necessary for the further development of the personality.

At this stage of Merton's life, we see that he is off to a bad start because he had lost his mother so early. He may have unconsciously felt that feminine love was unreliable; thus, having fruitful relationships with the opposite sex may prove problematic in the future (he will, indeed, have such difficulty), and he will also have difficulty connecting with his inner anima. Jung himself confessed that when his own emotional health was at stake, he always turned to his anima because he trusted the feminine side of his personality. For Merton, it is a different scenario; he employs the terms *anima* and *animus* in one of his journal entries, proving a familiarity with Jungian theory,[6] but it takes a long time for him to integrate his anima.

# Chapter Two

Life after his mother's death was not easy for Merton. His father could not find steady work and turned to his painting as his main occupation. Merton compares his father's early artistic style to that of Cézanne and his later style to the American painter John Marin. Owen Merton was in constant search of places to paint and decided to take along as his companion his older son Tom, leaving his younger son John Paul behind with his grandparents in Douglaston, on Long Island.

Thus, the young Merton began his nomadic wanderings with a father who seemingly was lost without his wife, a man himself in search of meaning, which he hoped to find in art. With his father, Merton traveled to Truro, Massachusetts, particularly the artist colony, Provincetown. Later, he accompanied him to Bermuda, living in a boarding house where, mostly unsupervised, he was often free to do as he pleased. Soon after, his father had a successful exhibit in New York while Merton remained in Bermuda with his father's friends.

> It is almost impossible to make much sense out of the continual rearrangement of our lives and our plans from month to month in childhood. Yet every new development came to me as a reasonable and worthy change. Sometimes I had to go to school, sometimes I did not. Sometimes Father and I were living together, sometimes I was with strangers and only saw him from time to time. People came into our lives

and went out of our lives. We had now one set of friends, now another. Things were always changing. I accepted it all. Why should it ever have occurred to me that nobody lived like that?[1]

Anyone who possesses the least bit of knowledge about child rearing knows this type of life is unstable for children who need a sense of security and structure to thrive. Fortunately, he later returned to the security and order of his grandparents' home while his father traveled to France to continue painting.

His father accomplishes some of his best paintings at this time, at the same time winning the attention of an important art critic, Roger Fry. He then returns to New York, and to his son's surprise, he sports a beard, to be followed by a greater surprise: His father is taking him to live in France. Merton falls in love with France, the land of his birth. His father not only wants to paint the French countryside, but he also hopes to make a home for his two boys. The two boys really have no home; homelessness became a theme often commented on by Merton. He is delighted when his father decides to build a house in France, but before this decision, Merton attends the normal school in Montauban, where he is a very unhappy student: "I knew for the first time in my life the pains of desolation and emptiness and abandonment."[2] It is not the first time he has felt this way; he experienced similar feelings when his mother died. He pleads with his father to take him out of the school; yet he has to remain: "The wound was no longer so raw: but I was never happy or at peace in the violent and unpleasant atmosphere of those brick cloisters."[3] What he desperately needed was a home, the absence of which his father hopes to fill.

In 1926 Merton again moves, this time to Murat, France, where he lives with a pious, loving family, the Privats, whom he describes as among "the most remarkable people I ever knew."[4]

They treat him with respect and affection, but they have the good sense to know the boy is wounded and do not attempt to get too close. Merton writes, "As a child, he's eleven now and since then too, I have always tended to resist any kind of possessive affection on the part of any other human being—there had always been this profound instinct to keep clear, to keep free. And only with supernatural people have I ever felt really at my ease, really at peace."[5] It is an extraordinary confession because it reveals the extent of his own woundedness: he mistrusts human, emotional touch. His fear of intimacy surely commenced with the loss of his mother; it is through the anima that a man possesses the Eros to connect with other people. Merton indeed loved the Privats, but the wounded boy could only love them from afar.

When his father returns from England, he begins to build a home for his two sons, but he suddenly decides to return to England, and, although the house is finished, they never live a single day in it. In England, young Merton stays with his beloved Aunt Maud, with whom he shared his secret desire to become a writer. A wise woman, she accepts his ambition but warns him that writing is a difficult life and that he should have a backup plan to support himself (good advice for *all* aspiring writers).

The most important issue at hand now is Merton's admission into a good English school. He briefly attended Ripley Court, but now at fourteen, he is too old for the school. Because he has little Latin (and his father has little money), public schools like Harrow or Winchester are out of the question. His Uncle Ben, however, comes up with a good solution, recommending a somewhat obscure but reputable school in the Midlands called Oakham.

During his time at Oakham (1929–33), Merton is an excellent student. Gifted in languages, he reads Molière, Racine, Balzac, Hugo, Goethe, and Schiller. He also enjoys reading modern novelists such as Gide, Dos Passos, Hemingway, Lawrence, and Jules Romain. His essay on the modern fictional hero wins him the Bailey English Prize.

During this time, his father would die of brain cancer. At school break, he and his father traveled to Scotland. But his father was so sick he left his son with friends to enter a hospital. Soon after, the young Merton receives a cryptic telegram, "Entering New York harbor. All well."[6] It was signed and stamped from London. Here is Merton's response to the telegram:

> I sat there in the dark, unhappy room, unable to think, unable to move, with all the innumerable elements of my isolation crowding in upon me from every side: without a home, without a family, without a country, without a father, apparently without any friends, without interior peace or confidence or light or understanding of my own—without God, too, without God, without heaven, without grace, without anything. And what was happening to Father, there, in London?[7]

The wounded boy is now even more wounded, again alone with no one to turn to. He later learns from his uncle that his father suffered from a malignant brain tumor.

If we analyze the above passage from an archetypal perspective, Merton is a sort of exiled Adam, a stranger in a strange land. His feelings of alienation are still with him when he enters the Abbey of Gethsemani in 1941:

> The sense of exile bleeds inside me like a hemorrhage—it is always the same *wound*, whether it is a sense of sin, or of loneliness, or of one's own insufficiency, or a spiritual dryness: they are all really the

same, in the way we experience them. In fact, spiritual dryness is one of the most acute experiences of longing we can have—therefore, of love.[8] (emphasis added)

Although now writing in theological language, he underscores his basic problem: He is still lonely, still feeling homeless. As a young man in his twenties, he still feels like a person in exile—still an orphan.

With his father's illness and imminent death, Merton finds himself lost in a dark wood of doubt, confusion, and guilt. Somehow he has to make sense of what appears to be a senseless world; he has to find answers to questions that seem to be unanswerable. He can make no sense out of his father's suffering: "There was no way for me, or for anyone else in the family, to get anything out of it. It was a raw wound for which there was no adequate relief. You had to take it, like an animal." Unaware of it at the time, he has embarked upon the "path that does not stray," which he later describes as an "interior journey."[9]

On one of his last visits to his father in the hospital, Merton finds his father's bed strewn with little sheets of blue paper with drawings similar to icons of Byzantine saints. The drawings puzzle the young son because his father is not a particularly religious man, his usual subjects for painting being representations of scenes from nature.

Merton speculates that within his father's cancer-ridden body lurked repressed spiritual longings. Later, as a converted Catholic and a monk, these remembered speculations serve as a consolation to Merton, hoping that his father, through his suffering, had found salvation. In a mysterious way his father's artistic renderings of Byzantine saints presage Merton's own soul making, brought to light when he first viewed the Byzantine mosaics of Christ on a trip to Rome, art that moved him to the core of his being.

For two months after his father's death, Merton is depressed. Stripped of everything that would impede the desires and wishes of his will, he can now do as he pleased: "The hard crust of my dry soul finally squeezed out all the last traces of religion that had ever been in it."[10] He describes his young self:

> I now belonged to the world in which I lived. I became a true citizen of my disgusting century: the century of poison gas and atomic bombing…a man with veins full of poison, living in death.[11]

Merton is obviously still filled with guilt and hatred, not only for himself but also for the world. His shadow archetype has overwhelmed him. Jung says the shadow is "the thing a person has no wish to be."[12] It consists of all those aspects of ourselves that we would rather not face or acknowledge: our imperfections, our capacity for evil, and the actual evil we have done—the memory of which we usually repress.

As a teenager, Merton is already wounded, lost, and confused, projecting his woundedness onto the world around him. His state of being is sad, to say the least.

Let us look more closely at Merton's description of himself. When he was a teenager, there was no atomic bomb. As to poison gas, he was probably referring to World War I. The atomic holocaust of World War II lay in the future, so the use of the word *disgusting* is suspect. Merton is surely engaged in a classic case of psychological projection onto his young, remembered self. Why would he feel so negatively about himself? Could it be that he felt that he himself was the *cause*, first of his mother's death of cancer, secondly his father's death of the same disease? Or is it that he considered himself a great sinner, like St. Augustine? One thing is certain: The syndrome of *contemptus mundi* to which Merton later admits has already taken root,[13] causing him to suffer from a spiritual malaise that he will eventually have to face, to accept, and to integrate if he is ever to achieve spiritual and psychological wholeness.

In the spring of 1932, Merton returns from a walking tour of Germany to his prep school Oakham. He cuts short his vacation (again he was alone) because of an infected toe. On return to school he develops an infected *tooth*. His body pulses with poisonous gangrene. After the school doctor extracts the tooth, he becomes sicker and is transferred to the infirmary. His doctor lances a hole in his gum to drain the infection. Merton describes his mouth as "full of filth."[14] He is in bad shape physically, psychologically, and spiritually: "But I now lay on this bed, full of gangrene, and my soul was rotten with the corruption of my sins. And I did not even care whether I died or lived."[15] Seventeen years old, and he cares not whether he lives or dies! It is a rather melodramatic comment from a most imaginative young man, but his self-description suggests a disturbed adolescent for whom, today, a family physician would swiftly recommend psychotherapy and the obligatory antidepressants.

What are these "sins" about which he laments? They are those of any other normal young man: drinking excessively, rowdy behavior with the guys, reading risqué novels, flirtations and kissing girls, all typical rites of passage for most young men (he later fathers a child while attending Cambridge, but this fact is not included in his autobiography).

His self-loathing goes deeper than fathering a child: It harkens back to his early childhood. Merton's mother had had high standards for her son. She observed his every movement, even to her recording his first words in "Tom's Book." She managed his education, cognizant of innovative, progressive educational theories. When she tried to teach her son to spell, the five-year-old kept spelling *which* without the first *h*. Impatient and strict, she sent him off to bed as punishment.

At an early age, perfection had been held up to him as an ideal, and when he failed to reach such perfection, there was punishment. That he remembers this "insignificant" event speaks very much about Merton the *boy*, and about Merton the man remembering his mother and childhood as he wrote his autobiography in the Abbey of Gethsemani.

In December of 1933, at seventeen, he wins a scholarship to Clare College, Cambridge. The day after his birthday, January 31, 1934, he embarks on a solo vacation to Italy, a journey that would change him forever. "So there I was, with all the liberty that I had been promising myself for so long. The world was mine. How did I like it? I was doing just what I pleased, and instead of being filled with happiness and well-being, I was miserable. The love of pleasure is destined by its very nature to defeat itself and end in frustration."[16]

Florence, Italy, being too cold, he sets out for Rome. He is a typical tourist, but he is actually more of a pilgrim in search of meaning. He begins to visit Rome's churches; he is fascinated by their Byzantine mosaics, discovering them to be not only beautiful but numinous. The huge icons of Christ, in particular, awe him. For the first time in his life, he truly wants to know "Who this Person was that men called Christ."[17] Simone Weil says that beauty is God's "trap" for men's souls.[18] Merton is now hooked, jerked out of his overpowering ego, and for the first time he wants to know God. He haunts the old Roman churches and their artistic treasures. To understand them and to learn more about Christ, he purchases a Vulgate Bible.

From a Jungian perspective, Merton is now well launched upon his journey to wholeness. For a brief time, religious beauty wrested him from himself, but gazing upon artistic renditions of Christ and *experiencing* Christ are two very different things. Merton surely yearns to be reborn, but this rebirth (his conversion to Catholicism) is still a long way off.

In his Roman hotel room, he experiences an extraordinary "paranormal" event: He feels the presence of his father in his room. He also feels pierced by a light, unveiling the condition of his soul. He is horrified, and this causes him to pray earnestly.

In Shakespeare's play *Hamlet*, the ghost father visits his son and demands revenge for his foul murder. But Merton's experience is quite a different visitation: The "presence" of his father is Merton's own shadow. How can the shadow communicate with a young man who is not listening, not living fully? Who seems bent on self-destruction? The shadow can communicate through the person Merton most admired: his beloved father. He is the only one Merton would listen to; thus, the message of the archetypal shadow through the father *finally* gets through to the young man. Merton then turns to prayer because he understands he needs the assistance of a "higher power" to face the dark side of his personality. He needs the Self, the unifying force of the psyche symbolically represented by his father, who, as previously mentioned, drew Byzantine faces on his deathbed—icons similar to the Byzantine mosaics that awed Merton in Rome.

Although his father's death is indeed a debilitating wound, its positive effect is that it launched Merton on his inner journey: He too must experience a death, the death of his ego-dominated personality.

Again, we question what such a young man could have done in his life to be "horrified" by it. The answer is (at least in part) that he is surely the victim of an inflated ego; thus, his sins are greater than anyone else's, a pride representing a kind of specialness, one that creates a hierarchy of sinners. Merton, like Stephen Daedalus in Joyce's *A Portrait of the Artist as a Young Man*, places himself at the top of the world's list of sinners: One of his mortal sins, he later states, could have caused World War II! This absurd idea, however, is *sincerely* felt by Merton. The important thing, though, is that he is now individuating, seeking answers to his unhappiness. In time he will realize that the ego is *not* the center of the psyche but that the Self, who for Western man is Christ, is the center.

The next part of Merton's journey entails his years at Clare College, Cambridge. Anyone who has visited both Cambridge and Oxford knows that each possesses its own unique charm and beauty. Some prefer the lily-white beauty of Cambridge, others the amber-chrysanthemum beauty of Oxford. Merton, however, loathed Cambridge. How could anyone hate such a lovely university town famous for its lush green quads, its beautiful marshes, and its flowing River Cam? How could one not rhapsodize over the fan vaulting of one of the most exquisite chapels in Christendom? Merton, however, saw none of Cambridge's beauty. For him it was a sort of hell on earth. He writes:

> Perhaps to you the atmosphere of Cambridge is neither dark nor sinister. Perhaps you were never there except in May. You never saw anything but the thin Spring sun half veiled in the mists and blossoms of the gardens along the Backs, smiling on the lavender bricks and stones of Trinity and St. John's or my own college Clare.
>
> I am even willing to admit that some people might live there for three years, or even a lifetime, so protected that they never sense the sweet stench of corruption that is all around them—the keen, thin, scent of decay that pervades everything and accuses with a terrible accusation the superficial youthfulness, the abounding undergraduate noise that fills those ancient buildings. But for me, with my blind appetites, it was impossible that I should not rush in and take a huge bite of this rotten fruit. The bitter taste is still with me after not a few years.[19]

Many readers are baffled by his negative description of Cambridge. Considering Merton's life at Cambridge, we can put the pieces together and understand why he grows to hate the place. He is wild and promiscuous at Cambridge and ultimately fathers a child. We first learn of the child in Monica Furlong's biography of Merton, later to be corroborated by Michael Mott's *The Seven Mountains of Thomas Merton.*

Merton's Augustinian exploits created a rift between him and his guardian and godfather Tom Bennett. It must have been difficult for Bennett to clean up the mess Merton had made of his life. We do not know the particulars of the financial settlement made with the young woman, and we do not know for sure what happened to her or the child. What *is* certain is that Merton always felt bad about the break in his relationship with his guardian. In his autobiographical novel *The Labyrinth*, he writes:

> And my godfather: I have left and not been able to make peace with him, nor tell him I am sorry so that he will believe it, or tell him I did not want to really do everything I did at Cambridge: that I did not want that aggregate of things, but something completely different, which of course I did not find, and could not, because I was too much of a fool in the first place, and too vain to understand anything except in terms of complete egoism.[20]

It should be noted that the rift between Merton and his guardian was never healed, but at one point Merton contacted Tom Bennett's widow, for it had been relayed to him that she felt that he had been unfair in his depiction of her husband in his autobiography. After an unsuccessful attempt to contact her in the mid-1950s, he was finally able to communicate with her, and there was explanation and reconciliation with her.

Was there something *else* that happened at Cambridge to make Merton loathe it so much? Michael Mott says, "It [Cambridge] is also personified into something like an animal, which gored him so deeply he felt that he would never entirely recover from the wound. What the wound was he never quite tells the reader."[21] But there is a hint of what that wounding might be in an interview with Merton and Harold Talbott in the latter's hut in Dharamsala. Talbott says,

> Merton helped me by telling me that when he was in an English university he had had an affair with the girl who made the beds in his dormitory, and she had a baby, and he said to me, 'You know my son would be such and such an age right now and I don't know whether he survived the blitz or not.' And he carried that with him. That was on his mind. And he let me know that this was the *key* to his life.[22] (emphasis added)

If one of the roots of Merton's hurt heart is his feeling that he was abandoned by his mother, did he not do the exact thing with his child? Of course, we know that his mother did not "abandon" Merton, but a child might indeed *feel* abandoned by a mother's death—he might even feel he was the *cause* of her death. Such feelings can affect a whole life. How would he feel about a young girl left alone with his child, in an England soon to be at war?

As to Merton's promiscuity, we can only assume it was the recklessness of an unhappy youth, one who had yet to come to terms with his shadow. When a person has begun to integrate his shadow, he is well on his way to psychological wholeness. Jung writes:

> When the ego and the shadow work in close harmony, the person feels full of life and vigor. The ego

channels instead of obstructing the forces emanating from the instincts. Consciousness is expanded and there is a liveliness and vitality to mental activity. And not only mental activity; the person is also physically more alive and vigorous.[23]

Merton says he took a "huge bite" (sexual imagery) of Cambridge, and we are again returned to archetypal imagery: the apple of the Garden of Eden. At this time his *contemptus mundi* grows harsh and expands to include *all* of England and for that matter Europe too. While at Cambridge, he was likely unconscious of his contempt of the world, but later when he became a monk, he admitted, "I had this simple *contemptus mundi* [contempt for the world]...the world was bad, the monastery good."[24] He explains:

But it seemed to me that there was some kind of subtle poison in Europe, something that corrupted me, something the very thought and scent of which sickened me, repelled me. What was it? Some kind of a moral fungus, the spores of which floated in that damp air, in that foggy and half-lighted darkness.[25]

Notice two things in this passage: He uses *passive* verbs: *is corrupted*, *sickened*, and *repelled* by something exterior to himself. He takes no responsibility for what renders him unhappy. It is the corrupt world. Thus, he is again caught in a classic example of psychological projection: First, it is Cambridge itself, then it is the whole of England, and finally it is all of Europe. He is the "victim" of all three; therefore, he is not responsible in his mind for the kind of person he has become. In his immaturity, he has failed to grasp the truth that the fault lies not in anything outside ourselves, "not in our stars but in ourselves."

The imagery of corruption, poison, moral fungus, fog, damp air, half-lit darkness are all reminiscent of T. S. Eliot's "The Waste Land"; at this point in Merton's life, he resembles Eliot's "Hollow Men." Paradoxically, from negativity and darkness (shadow) good *will* emerge because Merton is at least aware of his injury; he is very much Carl Jung's modern man in search of a soul, but even as a monk in 1946, he still execrates Cambridge:

> Oh read the verses of the loaded scourges,
> And what is written in their terrible remarks:
> "The Blood runs down the walls of Cambridge town,
> As useless as the waters of the narrow river—
> While pub and alley gamble for His vesture.
> …And yet with every wound You robbed me of a crime,
> And as each blow was paid with Blood,
> You paid me also each great win with greater graces.[26]

After his Aunt Maud's death in 1933, Merton's last close relative, Merton's life at Cambridge turns into a veritable orgy of drinking, dissipation, and girl chasing. His friends colorfully describe Merton's lifestyle at Cambridge: "he went off the rails," he was a "ship without an anchor," he "mucked with the wrong set," he went "wenching and drinking," and "debauchery is not too strong a word" for his behavior.[27]

From another perspective, we can say, "where sin abides, grace abounds" (Rom 5:20 KJV). Jung says that the journey to wholeness requires the thorn in the flesh; Merton had plenty of thorns. Jung writes:

> There is no light without shadow and no psychic wholeness without imperfection. To round itself out, life calls not for perfection but for completeness; and for

this the "thorn in the flesh" is needed, the suffering of defects without which there is no progress and ascent.[28]

At Cambridge, Merton manages to achieve only a second in Modern Language Tripos; nevertheless, he plans to continue his education at Clare College in the fall of 1934. However, in America on a visit to his maternal grandparents, he receives a letter from his guardian advising him to abandon his goal of entering the British Diplomatic Service, recommending his permanently remaining in America. Merton is relieved.

> The thought that I was no longer obliged to go back into those damp and fetid mists filled me with an immense relief—that far overbalanced the pain of my injured pride, the shame of comparative failure.[29]

Besides his sins of the flesh, Michael Mott suggests another reason for Merton's loathing of Cambridge. He gives an account of a party Merton attended where a mock crucifixion was reenacted, with Merton's playing the role of Christ. This event appears in Merton's unpublished novel *The Labyrinth*, written in 1939. Many years later, Merton's friend and literary agent Naomi Burton Stone noticed a scar on the palm of Merton's right hand. When she asked him about it, Merton awkwardly joked that it was his "stigmata."[30]

When he summarizes his life in England, he characteristically blames England, as well as the Europe, for the kind of person he has become:

> I was something that had been spawned by selfishness and irresponsibility of the materialistic century in which I lived. However, what I did not see was that my own age and class only had an accidental part to

play in this. They gave my egoism and pride and my other sins a peculiar character of weak and supercilious flippancy proper to this particular century, but that was only on the surface. Underneath, it was the same old story of greed and lust and self-love, of the three concupiscences bred in the rich, rotted undergrowth of what is technically called "the world" in every age, in every class.[31]

Again, Merton is the "victim": He is acted upon by outside forces over which he has no control. Whereas before it was Cambridge, then Europe, now it is his class and its customs that have made him the person he is. He also faults *all* wealthy people as lustful and egotistic, and "the world" is "rotted undergrowth." Here, in short, is his fullest expression of his *contemptus mundi*. It is really not that much different from Hamlet's description of Denmark as an "unweeded garden that grows to seed. Things rank and gross in nature possess it merely."[32]

There is *one* positive aspect of the above projection: It indicates a transition. At first, he faults huge entities like the city of Cambridge, the country England, and the Continent. He is now turning from huge abstractions to people—in particular the upper class. If he continues this declension, he will end up where he should: with *himself*. When he arrives at that point, he will by thorough self-analysis begin to "own" his projections and then integrate them, and, like Shakespeare's Prospero referring to Caliban, he will be able to say, "This thing of darkness I acknowledge my own."[33]

# Chapter Three

Back in America, Merton resides with his maternal grandparents in Douglaston, on New York's Long Island. Although his life in Cambridge had been a disaster area, Merton is still a fortunate person in that not too many young men are given second chances after fathering children out of wedlock. He does not have to abandon his education by marrying and supporting a wife and child. Merton's social position, upper middle class because of his grandfather's money and influence, offers him a second chance. However, he fails to transform himself as quickly as he might have.

Merton's first psychological order of business is to decide upon which persona (Latin for "mask") to adopt in his "new" country. Merton has the opportunity to become a far different person, a more mature and responsible one, but he decides, to his later dismay, to retain, in his repertoire of personae, masks he should have abandoned. In fact, Merton dabbles with so many personae that he could cry, like King Lear, "Who is it that can tell me who I am?"[1] When one is caught up in the donning and mixing of so many masks, one loses touch with the True Self, a concept to become a major preoccupation of Thomas Merton, or rather "Father Louis," Cistercian monk.

It should be noted that Merton was well aware of Jung's concept of personae. Merton writes, "When I take the beer cans to the dump this morning, I will also take the following masks: the monastic failure, the *poète maudit*; the ex-priest alcoholic driven to drink by M; the loner misunderstood by everyone; and I might as well add the wild faun bit while at it."[2]

Experimenting with too many masks, one can lose sight of who one really is, and if one overidentifies with one particular mask, one may find oneself doing things not faithful to the True Self. Jung writes, "One could say, with a little exaggeration, that the persona is that which in reality one is not, but which oneself as well as others think one is."[3]

The vocational mask that Merton hopes to adopt in America is that of journalist, and he was advised that a college degree would be helpful toward that end. He enrolls at Columbia University in February of 1935 and quickly makes a number of new friends, immersing himself in a whirl of activity including, besides academic courses, parties, drinking, dating, sports, attending jazz sessions, and pledging a fraternity. He also joins the literary magazine *The Jester* where he meets people who become his lifetime friends, notably Robert Lax and Ed Rice; in addition, he also works for other campus publications: the *Spectator* and the *Columbia Review*, where he meets his future champion for his autobiography, Robert Giroux, publisher extraordinaire, and the doomed poet John Berryman. His political persona entails a brief flirtation with the Young Communist League, adopting the party name Frank Swift; but he is disenchanted after attending one meeting.

In a short time, Merton is a "big man on campus," persisting, however, in activities that reinforce his persona of the sexual athlete and the heavy drinker, to the point that his college fraternity, dazzled by Merton's sybaritic lifestyle, often refers to him as "our Merty." How much of a rake Merton actually was we perhaps may never know, but one thing is certain: Merton finds himself just as unhappy and unfulfilled in America as he was in England. At Columbia, however, Merton earns his BA and MA in English.

Then his beloved grandfather Sam Jenkins dies. He has already lost so many of his relatives: his mother, his father, his Aunt Maud. He also lost his relationship with godfather/guardian Tom Bennett, and now the family's patriarchal anchor is dead. *This* death brings him to the edge of a nervous collapse. On a train going into Manhattan from Douglaston, Merton suffers an attack of vertigo. Making his way to the passageway between train cars for fresh air, he has another attack, which tempts him to fall to the tracks below and thus to certain death. He holds on for dear life, and when he reaches Penn Station, he immediately checks himself into the Pennsylvania Hotel, swiftly summoning the house doctor to examine him. Merton never forgot that day:

> I lay on the bed and I listened to the blood pounding rapidly inside my head. I could hardly keep my eyes closed. Yet I did not want to open them, either. I was afraid that if I even looked at the window, the strange spinning inside my head would begin again.
>
> That window! It was huge. It seemed to go right down to the floor. Maybe the force of gravity would draw the whole bed, with me on it, to the edge of that abyss, and spill me headlong into the emptiness.
>
> And far, far away in my mind was a little, dry, mocking voice that said: "What if you threw yourself out of the window...." I thought to myself, "I wonder if I am having a nervous breakdown."[4]

In my estimation, this portion of Merton's autobiography has not been sufficiently examined. To me it is an outright admission to suicidal longing. He has come to America to start anew, and in a hotel room "a mocking voice" whispers, "What if you threw yourself out of the window?" It is *Merton's* voice; it is *Merton's* thought, it is *Merton's* despair. Merton has again failed to turn his life around. He indeed had many friends (and several girlfriends), and he is actively involved in Columbia's social life, but he is still miserable. He corroborates this "nervous breakdown" in an October 22, 1952, journal entry:

> Since my retreat I have been having another one of those nervous breakdowns. The same old familiar business. I am getting used to it now—since the old days in 1936, when I thought I was going to crack up on the Long Island Railroad, and the more recent one since ordination.[5]

Not addressing his mental state (perhaps unqualified to do so), his family doctor (a general practitioner) diagnoses a case of severe gastritis, bordering on ulcers. He prescribes medicine and a special diet. Today, of course, an astute doctor would have advised psychological therapy as quickly as possible, as well as a referral to a psychiatrist.

As for his gastritis, we today know enough about psychosomatic illness to understand that Merton's physical problems quite possibly reflected a disturbed mind and soul. He was suffering from existential angst and from guilt (likely the guilt of fathering and abandoning his child).

Around this same time, Merton experienced another setback. He fell into a love affair that ended with his being summarily rejected by a woman who, he felt, humiliated and wounded him. He wrote, "The *wounds* within me were, I suppose, enough. I was bleeding to death" (emphasis added).[6]

As suggested, if a male child undergoes a negative maternal experience, it may adversely affect his relationships with other women for the rest of his life, and he will likely distrust the feminine—a distrust also of himself because he too carries within him his own inner woman (the anima of which Jung speaks).

During his young adult life, Merton repeatedly fails to establish a lasting relationship with the opposite sex. He may have unconsciously feared another abandonment by a woman (like his mother's). He may have even feared intimacy lest he sire another heir; thus, he severs relationships before he can be hurt. No relationship, consequently, blossoms into a healthy, nurturing one. Or it may have been more complicated. On the eve of his fiftieth birthday, Merton attempts to understand his problem with the opposite sex:

> I suppose I regret my lack of love, my selfishness and glibness (covering a deep shyness and need for love) with girls who, after all, did love me, I think, for a time. My great fault was my inability to get complete assurance and perfect fulfillment.[7]

Remembering the women in his life, Merton recalls one in particular: "When I came to the monastery, Ginny Burton remained as the symbol of the girl I ought to have fallen in love with but didn't and she remains the image of one I really did love, with a love of companionship, and not of passion."[8]

At the end of part 1 of his autobiography, Merton admits to feeling completely defeated: His life, it seemed, was a "blind alley."[9] A dead end. But as the poet Theodore Roethke reminds us, "In a dark time the eye begins to see."[10] Merton's dark time paradoxically serves as the occasion for his rescue.

The problem, simply stated, is that Merton must somehow find a reliable woman, one who accepts him along with his shadow, which often makes him feel miserable as well as suicidal. Merton's life somewhat mirrors T. S. Eliot's prophetic verse that the only hope of empty men is the "perpetual star" and "the multifoliate rose"—that is, Mary, the mother of God, and Holy Mother Church.

In the meantime, Merton needs mentors, or at least *a* mentor. He is lost without Tom Bennett, who was like a father to him in England. Now he must find the necessary guides to lead him through his hell of confusion, as Virgil led Dante through the Inferno to Beatrice. As Merton was spiritually inspired by art in Rome, he is now similarly moved and influenced by great writers. This is, of course, not surprising because Merton longed to be a writer himself. Logos, the "word," it seems, dominates Merton's life. Jung says Logos is a principle characteristic of men. It entails judgment and discrimination: "Logos is essential reason. Each person, therefore, has his own Logos which connects him, ultimately, with meaning."[12]

A few of the writers from whom Merton seeks meaning are Étienne Gilson, Aldous Huxley, William Blake, and Gerard Manley Hopkins. Each offers to him some ray of insight, ultimately illuminating Merton's way into the Catholic Church.

In February of 1937, while walking by Scribner's Fifth Avenue bookshop, Merton notices in its window display Étienne Gilson's book, *The Spirit of Medieval Philosophy*. He has a little money to burn a hole in his pocket, so he purchases the book and begins reading it on the train home. When he notices the book's *Imprimatur* ("let it be printed") and *Nihil Obstat* ("nothing stands in the way"), he is disgusted and nearly throws the book out the window. Though capable of appreciating Catholic churches and art, Merton remains biased about the Catholic Church—perhaps the result of his grandfather's virulent anti-Catholic sentiments. Surely being educated in England—a nation separated from the church since Henry VIII, with an anti–Roman Church bias in its very being—is probably another factor in his negative attitude about the Catholic Church.

Gilson's book explains to Merton the philosophical and theological foundation of Catholicism, whose symmetry, beauty, and profundity he finds as luminous and moving as the mosaics he fell in love with in Rome.

He reads about a concept of God that intellectually satisfies him, the concept of *Aseitas*: It "made a profound impression on me that I made a pencil note at the top of the page: 'Aseity of God—God is being *per se*'."[13] God is *pure* Being, existing always in, of, by itself. This concept revolutionizes Merton's intellectual and spiritual life.

Another book also comes his way, recommended to him by his new Columbia friend Robert Lax: Aldous Huxley's *Ends and Means*. It introduces Merton to two spiritual ways of life: asceticism and mysticism.

> Asceticism! The very thought of such a thing was a complete revolution to my mind….What an idea! To deny the desires of one's flesh and even to practice certain disciplines that punished and mortified those desires until this day, these things had never succeeded in giving me anything but gooseflesh. But of course Huxley did not stress the physical angle of mortification and asceticism—and that was right, in so far as he was more interested in striking to the very heart of the matter, and showing the ultimate positive principle underlying detachment.[14]

Merton is likely attracted to asceticism perhaps because he has too often been the victim of his own concupiscence. Like Augustine, he too could have cried out to God, "Grant me chastity and self-control, but please not yet."[15] He is also drawn to the possibility of detachment and discipline as a means toward liberating himself from desire so that the True Self could be experienced. Such a possibility causes another "revolution" in his mind. The world of mysticism, about which Huxley so eloquently writes, opens Merton to the hope of experiencing God in this life. Huxley writes at length about such Catholic mystics as Teresa of Avila, John of the Cross, and Meister Eckhart. They soon exert a far-reaching influence on Merton, one lasting a lifetime (he later wrote a book on St. John of the Cross). Huxley also stimulated Merton's interest in Buddhism, an interest that would fully blossom in the 1960s.

There are also two influential poets: William Blake and Gerard Manley Hopkins. We can never underestimate the influence of these poets—the first introduced to Merton by his father, the latter by a headmaster.

Merton's study of Blake becomes a joy and a grace. As a boy, he struggled with Blake's obscurity, but now as a man it is leading him to God. At Columbia, he writes his thesis on Blake. The first chapter of his most popular book contains a line taken from Blake, "Everything that is, / Is Holy." By the time he finishes his study of Blake, Merton knows he needs a vital faith to base his life on; it is the only way to live in a world that is charged with the presence and reality of God.

Merton also loved the poet Gerard Manley Hopkins from his Oakham days. Both had much in common: They are intellectuals, converts, and poets attracted to the idea of perfection in a Religious order. Merton is drawn to the simplicity of the Franciscan order, and Hopkins is drawn to the more intellectual orders of the Benedictines and the Jesuits. The more he reads of Hopkins, the more he thinks about his life as a Jesuit (Hopkins's preferred order), wondering what it would be like to be a priest. We can imagine Merton's reading and being moved by Hopkins's poem "The Habit of Perfection," whose opening verse became the title of the English version of Merton's autobiography, *Elected Silence*, a title chosen by another Catholic convert and novelist, Evelyn Waugh.

In a December 27, 1958, journal entry, Merton writes, "The end of a year—and the beginning of a very grave year of struggle, Christ, may I not go under. I understand now Hopkins' last sonnets. Does religious life do this to everyone sensitive?"[16] Anyone who has read what are commonly known as Hopkins's "terrible sonnets," written by the poet when he was teaching at University College in Dublin, knows they are poems of heart-wrenching despair. The poet was caught in an agonizing "dark night of the soul," but that phrase does not necessarily mean what St. John of the Cross meant. Today people often use the saint's expression to mean a very deep depression, and Merton at the time was almost surely referring to depression.

While writing his master's thesis, Merton reads another book that profoundly moves him, Jacques Maritain's *Art and Scholasticism.* He is becoming more and more attracted to Catholicism, discovering in Maritain a sane conception of virtue—without which, Maritain contends, there can be no happiness, because virtues are the powers by which we can become happy, for without them, life is joyless.

In addition to great art and great books, there are also some wonderful people who "sang" Merton into the church: Robert Lax, Ed Rice, Robert Gibney, Sy Freedgood, and, of course, Professor Mark Van Doren, whose course on Shakespeare, Merton says, is the best course he has ever taken, and the one that does him the most good. But of all his friends the one who exerts the greatest influence is Robert Lax, with whom he remains close until his death. Lax is a combination of Hamlet and Elias. He is Jewish, but like Merton, he too later converts to the Catholic Church. What Lax offers Merton is unconditional love, accepting Merton as well as implicitly trusting him.

By the beginning of September 1938, the groundwork for Merton's conversion is more or less complete. It requires a little more than a year and a half from his reading of Gilson for Merton to reject atheism and become a person open to the immense range and possibility of religious experience. He is ready ("readiness is all"—*Hamlet*) and ripe ("ripeness is all"—*King Lear*) for conversion. He has developed an appreciation of Catholic theology, an attraction to asceticism and mysticism, and he sorely craves love and forgiveness as well as a life of virtue. He just needs a gentle push, and it comes, of course, through a book.

On an October day in 1938, Merton is engrossed in G. F. Lahey's biography of Gerard Manley Hopkins. When he arrives at the section when Hopkins finally decides to seek John Henry Newman's help to convert to Catholicism, Merton impulsively jumps from his seat to rush to Corpus Christi Church near Columbia to inform Father George Ford that he wants to be accepted into the Catholic Church.

After a month of instruction from Father Moore, Merton is baptized on November 16, 1938, with Ed Rice, his only Catholic friend at Columbia, serving as his godfather. Thus, Thomas Merton has finally found a worthy recipient for his anima projection: Holy Mother Church. Through baptism, Merton is reborn as a Christian; on the same day he receives his first communion. Baptism cleanses him of a lifetime of sins. His conversion solves (temporarily) his anima problem by finding him a bride in the church, and the sacrament of baptism silences (temporarily) his shadow. He is a new man.

Jung understood the profound significance of Christian baptism:

> Baptism endows the human being with a unique soul...the idea of baptism lifts a man out of his archaic identification with the world and changes him into a being who stands above it. The fact that mankind has risen to the level of this idea is baptism

in the deepest sense, for it means the birth of spiritual man who transcends nature.[17]

Merton had come to his life's fork in the road, and he chose the one "less traveled by." He felt that he had walked into a "tremendous gravitational movement which is love, which is the Holy Spirit, and he felt he was loved: 'And He called out to me from His own immense depths'."[18]

"Cradle Catholics" often wonder about friends who have converted to their faith, "Did the conversion *take*?" In other words was it *lasting*? There are a number of famous twentieth-century converts to Catholicism, but they sometimes become what is known as "lapsed Catholics." Others become faithful members, like the poet Siegfried Sassoon who converted in later life, and ever afterwards experienced great peace. Clare Booth Luce is another example: She became a staunch Catholic convert, as did Waugh. There is also the famous case of Graham Greene, a convert many have wondered about: Was he *truly* Catholic? This question intrigues many of his readers.

Merton's conversion "took," but it is a bumpy journey after his conversion. He returned to his life of drinking, partying, and dating, putting himself too near occasions of sin. But he never abandons going to Mass, and this very practice may well have saved him. Carl Jung has a great respect for the mystery of the Mass and its power upon the individual. He writes:

The Mass is an extramundane and extratemporal act in which Christ is sacrificed and then resurrected in the transformed substances; and this rite of his sacrificial death is not a repetition of the historical event but the original, unique and eternal act. The experience of the Mass is therefore a participation in the transcendence of life, which overcomes all bounds of space and time.[19]

Two important events occur after Merton's conversion. First, Merton begins to write poetry. The second is a comment by his friend Robert Lax. Merton mentions to Lax that he wants to be a good Catholic. Lax gently chastises him, saying that he should *want* to be a saint. Lax's remark is a shock to Merton, and he offers a number of reasons why he cannot become a saint. But Lax wisely refutes him, saying that one need only to *want* to be a saint to become one. Unconvinced, Merton later mentions it to Mark Van Doren, who, to Merton's surprise, supports Lax.

Shortly afterwards, Merton purchases the *Works of St. John of the Cross*, and in his Perry Street room, he begins to acquaint himself with the great mystic, an initial reading that one day leads Merton to write a book about the saint and his mystical, dark way.

Later, in that very same Perry Street room, Merton announces to a group of friends, "I am going to be a priest."[20] Keep in mind that he has been reading a goodly amount of Hopkins, both his poetry and his notebooks. He has also read a book about the Jesuit order, and the idea of becoming a priest takes root in his mind. If Merton can, to borrow Jung's phrase, be described as a man in search of a soul, we can say he has already accomplished it. Merton is now a man in search of meaning, to borrow Victor Frankl's phrase, one that applies directly to his life. He wants to "do" something meaningful with his life, but he again slides into its usual habits of too much smoking, too much drinking, and too much socializing. He writes, "My whole life was at a crisis."[21]

His friends are skeptical about his becoming a priest, except for Dan Walsh, a philosophy teacher who teaches part-time at Columbia. Dan says, "You know, the first time I met you I thought you had a vocation to the priesthood."[22] (Dan himself would also become a priest.) Merton is astonished and begins to discuss Religious orders. Merton knows what he needs: an order that offers solitude and one based on a rule. Dan recommends the Benedictines and the Franciscans. The Franciscans follow a rule, faithful to St. Francis's simple and lyrical spirit. And the Benedictines, of course, follow the Rule of Saint Benedict, their spiritual father.

When Dan begins to speak about the Trappist order (a stricter reformed order of Cistercians—themselves a reform of the Benedictines), Merton shivers at the mere mention of the severe order. Six years before, Merton had once daydreamed about becoming a Trappist, but the very idea "almost reduced me to jelly."[23] Dan speaks of his attending a retreat at a Trappist monastery in Kentucky, Our Lady of Gethsemani, explaining their life of *ora et labora* (pray and work) and asceticism. When Dan asks Merton outright if such a life could interest him, Merton flat out says, "It would kill me in a week."[24]

In the end, Merton applies to the Franciscans. Having already taught English at their St. Bonaventure College, outside Buffalo, New York, he is quickly accepted as a candidate and is already imagining himself as a Franciscan monk wearing the brown robe, white cincture (rope belt), and leather sandals. Merton suffers a case of religious scrupulosity, however, and feels compelled to inform the Franciscans of his dissolute past, including his fathering a child. The order then asks him to withdraw his application. It is a terrible blow to Merton, reducing him to tears.

Why did Merton succumb to a compulsion to reveal his unsavory past to the Franciscans? He has confessed his past in the sacrament of penance and received absolution, everything has been wiped clean by baptism, penance, and grace given in holy communion. Merton likely did not forgive *himself*, unconsciously punishing himself by revealing his past to the

Franciscans. He has a pattern to follow: Was not his mother a severe taskmaster? Did she not send him to bed for stubbornly spelling a word incorrectly? Wasn't her ideal of perfection instilled in him?

By revealing his past to the Franciscans, he denies himself his most intense desire: to become a priest (or at least a *Franciscan* priest). Their rejection depresses him. He says, "It seemed to me that I was now excluded from the priesthood forever."[25]

From a Jungian perspective, Merton's actions are indicative of his failure to integrate his shadow archetype. Christ says, "Love your neighbor as you love yourself" (Matt 19:19). It may be that Merton is still filled with self-hatred. Although cleansed of his past sins through the sacraments, he has not forgiven himself, and to punish himself, he denies (unconsciously) his heart's desire: to become a priest.

Later, Merton follows Dan Walsh's suggestion to go on retreat at the Trappists in Kentucky. He falls in love with the abbey, saying, "This is the center of all the vitality that is in America."[26] Back at St. Bonaventure College he talks with one of the friars, asking him if fathering a child is an insurmountable obstacle to his becoming a priest. Father Philotheus suggests it should not be an impediment.

In 1941 war is imminent for America, and Merton has already been rejected by the draft (he had too few teeth). But he can be called again. He quickly writes to Gethsemani. On December 10, 1941, Merton arrives at the gates of the Abbey of Our Lady of Gethsemani where he asks entry into the Trappist order. At nearly twenty-seven years old, he is accepted as a postulant. As he passes through the abbey gate, he walks under a statue of Mary as Our Lady of Victory, below which is the salutation, "Peace," to be followed by another chiseled motto: "God Alone."

# Chapter Four

Upon entering Gethsemani on an overcast day in December 1941, Merton stepped back into medieval monastic life. Located in the remote hills of Kentucky, a harsh country, stupefyingly hot in summer and frigid in winter, Gethsemani is the first Cistercian foundation in America, established in 1849.

Life at Gethsemani is lived according to the Rule of St. Benedict, a rigorous, austere life based upon manual labor and prayer, the very kind of life Merton yearned for as a convert to the Catholic faith. Most monastic prayer is known as *lectio divina*, demanding *hours* of daily communal worship. Monks rise at 2 a.m. for Vigils; they retire after Compline at 7 p.m. And in between they pray Matins, Lauds, Prime, Terce, Sext, Nones, and Vespers as well as the Holy Mass! They wear black and white habits with cowls and work as well as sleep in them. Monks reside in one long dormitory divided by partitions, creating monastic cells with a curtain as a door, permitting little privacy. Each cell contains one wooden bed with a straw mattress, a crucifix, and a stoup for holy water hung on the wall. Their diet is vegetarian; meat, fish, and eggs are strictly forbidden. During Advent and Lent, the monks fast.

At first, Merton glories in such a life, fervently believing it would purge him of his past and transform him into a saint, the goal of every Catholic, as suggested to him by his best friend Robert Lax. Merton, however, already possessed a streak of perfectionism (inherited from his mother), but he discovers that the speedy transformation that he expected monastic life to offer does not materialize. Karen Horney (whom Merton had read) notes, "A person obsessed by a need for perfection largely loses his sense of proportion…the function of these trends can be better understood if we take a look at their genesis. They develop early in life through the combined effect of given temperamental and environmental influences."[1]

A healthier goal for Merton might have been for him to learn to accept himself, but as his monastic journals reveal, he is very much a divided man, still pursuing the *ignis fatuus* of perfection, a pursuit that would for years cause him much frustration, depression, and unhappiness.

He admits both in his autobiography and in his journal, *The Sign of Jonas*, to have been followed into Gethsemani by this shadow, his double, the writer. He says, "I brought all the instincts of a writer with me into the monastery, and I knew that I was bringing them, too. It was not a case of smuggling them in…I wanted to write poems and reflections and other things that came into my head in the novitiate."[2] At the same time, he wants to be a pure contemplative, disappearing into God. He battles this dual desire during the first years of his monastic life, capturing his thoughts and feelings in a journal begun on the fifth anniversary of his entry into Gethsemani, called *The Whale and the Ivy*. It was from this longer journal that Merton extracted his published journal, *The Sign of Jonas*, in 1953.

It is not only his shadow-writer that he brings into Gethsemani. He also brings along his archetypal shadow and its commensurate *contemptus mundi*, both of which remain his constant companions for many years. His shadow is so clearly evident in his book *Seeds of Contemplation* (published in 1949). He later disavows portions of what he said about the world, rewriting and expanding it into *New Seeds of Contemplation* in 1961.

His abbot, Dom Frederic Dunne, is a wise man. He sees that Merton is a gifted young man, a born writer, and decides to permit the young author (already a published poet) to express this integral part of his personality; to do otherwise would be wasteful and likely psychologically harmful for the young man. Consequently, he encourages Merton to write. Although Merton performs his fair share of manual labor, this work along with his writing proved too strenuous, bringing him close to a physical collapse.

Concerned about Merton's health, Abbot Dunne frees him from physical labor to allow him to pursue a more intellectual life, at the same time assigning to him several writing projects involving Cistercian history and hagiography. Around 1944, he also encourages Merton to write his autobiography. Merton has written several autobiographical novels, all sent to (and refused) by his Columbia peer Robert Giroux. He now turns to writing straightforward autobiography. By October 1946, Merton has sent his manuscript of *The Seven Storey Mountain* (the title is taken from Dante, whom he discovered while attending Cambridge) to his agent Naomi Burton. She is able to sell it to Giroux, who found it to be a gripping story.

Merton, however, remains ambivalent about his writing; he believes it interferes with his *true* purpose: to become a contemplative and to live as the motto over the Gethsemani entrance proclaims, for "God Alone."

It is difficult for people today to sympathize with Merton's dilemma because the solution is so seemingly obvious: The ability to write is a gift from God; therefore, by writing, one is following God's will. Why Merton did not understand this sentiment is an enigma, but it was not a rare problem. Merton's poetic hero, Gerard Manley Hopkins, considered writing poetry as an *obstacle* to his life as a Jesuit. Both men, however, *needed* the outlet of writing (Merton finally admits the need for this outlet in later journals) because they were supersensitive to their inward and outward lives, and felt compelled to write about what they saw and thought. They were men who truly exemplified the Greek ideal, "An unexamined life is not worth living."

Reading his second journal, one gathers that the first years, up to 1946, were a honeymoon period for Merton, when Merton's one desire was for solitude into which he hoped to be lost in the secrecy of God's face (yet it is odd that he destroyed his postulant journals). He later begins to complain to Abbot Dunne that he feels that he should become a Carthusian, perhaps the strictest of all monastic orders. Off and on during his whole career as a Trappist, he believes he should have entered the Carthusian order. His abbot and confessors all suggest that such an idea should be dismissed as temptation from the devil.

The other conflict concerns his writing: He is ambivalent about it. He considers it an obstacle to his becoming a pure contemplative—yet he wants to write. Actually he *cannot* cease writing because his abbot *ordered* him to write! There are occasions, however, when he longs not to write. Even journal writing, for which be became famous, he sometimes finds tedious, but because he has such an active mind, the journal serves as the perfect genre for his kind of thinking, often kindled by his reading, which was enormous.

The true purpose of Merton's life in the 1940s is not writing his autobiography or other books, but to become a priest. He makes his simple vows (of poverty, chastity, obedience, and stability) on March 19, 1944, and his solemn vows on March 19, 1947. A year later his beloved Abbot Dunne died, and a year after on May 26, 1949, he was ordained to the priesthood.

His assessment of himself the day before his priestly ordination reads:

> The truth is, I am far from being the monk or the cleric
> that I ought to be. My life is a great mess and tangle of
> half-conscious subterfuges to evade grace and duty. I

have done all things badly. I have thrown away great opportunities. My infidelity to Christ, instead of making me shudder, drives me on to throw myself all the more blindly on His mercy. I dare to go to the altar and say Mass after the way I have treated my other obligations, at least interiorly, in the past two or three years.[3]

It is surely a harsh indictment of himself. His shadow is again overwhelming him, but not completely, for by the end of the journal entry, he asserts his belief that becoming a priest will be his happiness and salvation. Of course, a vocation is an answer to God's call. It is *also* an answer to the call of the individuation process. Jolande Jacobi writes, "One might say that in the course of the individuation process a man arrives at the entrance to the house of God...for individuation is a psychological goal and not a religious one, although it can be reached only by including a religious attitude."[4]

Without a doubt, the zenith of Merton's life is his priesthood. Considering the early obstacles, it is miraculous that Merton actually becomes a priest. Today it is unlikely that a seminary would take Merton as a candidate if it knew his whole story of fathering a child. Would he have passed the battery of psychological tests and interviews every prospective priest today must endure before he is accepted as a seminarian?

He has no journal entry for the day of his ordination, the feast of the Ascension. His comments appear on May 29, after three days of festival. Celebrating his first Low and later that day Solemn Mass, Merton is awed and feels transformed. His best friends Lax, Walsh, Rice, and Giroux are there for the celebration. He writes, "The Mass is the most wonderful thing that has ever entered into my life."[5] It seems at this point in his life that Merton has it all; he is a monk, a best-selling writer (*The Seven Storey Mountain* had been published in 1948 to great success), and now a priest. All his dreams, it seems, have now come true. But as we shall see, he is at the threshold of a number of problems.

The main obstacle to what he calls his "progress" is the massive amount of writing in which he is involved. Even journal writing, for which he would become famous, is, as mentioned, considered "tedious." His journals are full of his prayers to God: "You will heal me when You will, because I have trusted You. I will not wound myself anymore with the details with which I have surrounded myself like thorns—a penance which You do not desire of me."[6] The "details" are likely the number of writing projects he has started. Because he is so busy being a writer, he has less time for prayer, and he is *disgusted* (his word) with himself: "I am content that these pages show me to be what I am: noisy, full of the racket of imperfections and passion and the wide open wounds left by sin, full of faults and envies and miseries and full of my own intolerable emptiness."[7] To his chagrin, he has not transformed himself and has not solved his "racket of imperfections," "wounds," and "envies."

*Seeds of Contemplation* follows his best-selling autobiography, but Merton is not pleased with it, or more accurately, he is ambivalent about it. He considers it too "cold and cerebral," lacking "warmth and human affection." Yet at another time he commented that it is one of his books that he would stand by even though he admits that he made a "stupid" remark about the Sufis.

Today critics are also split about it. Michael Mott, Merton's biographer, sees the book as a masterpiece of spiritual writing, while William Shannon describes it as an immature and naïve book. The truth is that it is both: It contains passages of beautiful prose along with profound and insightful counsel about the spiritual journey, but it is also marred by Merton's unintegrated shadow and *contemptus mundi*.

Soon after the publication of *Seeds*, Merton himself realizes that it contains passages overtly revealing his shadow projection, and he tones them down when he revises it. In the early 1960s, he renames it *New Seeds of Contemplation*. A good example of a passage that requires editing is this:

> Do everything you can to avoid the amusements and the noise and the business of men. Keep as far as you can from the places where they gather to cheat and insult one another, to exploit one another, to laugh at one another, or to mock one another with their false gestures of friendship. Do not read their newspapers, if you can help it. Be glad if you can keep beyond the reach of their radios. Do not bother with their unearthly songs or their intolerable concerns for the way their bodies look and feel.[8]

The passage is longer in its denunciation of the world. The signs of true spiritual (and psychological) "progress," to use Merton's word, however, are acceptance and compassion for the world, for one's brothers and sisters, even if they are great sinners. A "progressed" Christian practices the kind of compassion Christ offers to us by his example: he who forgave those who crucified him.

Compassion for the world outside Gethsemani is not easy for Merton because he has yet to integrate his own shadow and wounds. He has yet to forgive *himself* for his past life. It still haunts him; he has not forgotten abandoning the woman who bore his child (not dissimilar to what St. Augustine had done). Tom Bennett attended to the financial settlement, but Merton never settled this pivotal youthful event within his own mind and soul. He never definitively found out what happened to them, although it was presumed they both died in the blitz of England during World War II (but there is no actual proof of it).

He hopes that the stark, austere, harsh life of penance he lives at Gethsemani will transform him into the person he longs to be—a saint. He even dreams of sainthood: "Last night I dreamt I was telling several other monks, 'I shall be a saint,' and they did not seem to question me. Furthermore, I believed it myself. If I do—(I shall)—it will be because of the prayers of other people."[9]

He has yet to learn to live in the present moment (it would take a dose of Zen Buddhism to teach him this lesson), to accept himself (it would take much self-examination as well as analysis of his dreams), and finally to submit himself totally to God's will (he periodically accomplishes this submission but his strong will is always present). As for being a *saint*, Merton finally accepts the wisdom of leaving such things to God. To want to become a saint is truly a prideful desire, and Merton learns that peace of mind and soul lies in self-acceptance.

Thus, while becoming a priest and writing his book of thoughts on what it means to be a contemplative, Merton himself remains an *alienated* man, angry at himself and at the world, and still rejecting both. Here is another passage he becomes somewhat ashamed of:

> I have very little idea of what is going on in the world, but occasionally I happen to see some of the things they are drawing and writing there and it gives me the conviction that they are all living in *ash cans*. It makes me glad I cannot hear what they are singing.[10]

The very use of such an extremely negative image for the world, "ash cans," suggests that Merton is still trapped by a rather powerful, unconscious emotion; thus, in keeping the world at a distance, he also keeps at a distance (buried in the unconscious) his own shadow. The image of ash cans is, actually, an apt metaphor for the unconscious. As we toss the debris of our daily life into the ash can, so too do we often relegate negative aspects about ourselves into the ash can of our unconscious, aspects that Jung refers to as the archetypal shadow.

In this excerpt, Merton, however, is disingenuous. He has not forgotten the world where he had wildly lived, relishing, and reveling in its pleasures, and he still vividly remembers his Cambridge days that have not faded in the least, although he may not yet have taken full responsibility for them. Even in a poem he wrote in 1949, his Cambridge wounds are still very much on his mind:

> They have given the cricketer a grass heart
> And a dry purse like a leaf, Look!
> Look! The little butterflies come out!
> He was wounded, he was wounded in the wars
> Where the roots our umpires are.[11]
>
> "Sports Without Blood—A Letter to
> Dylan Thomas," 1948

They were days and wounds that paradoxically brought him to Christ. The memory of those days are also caught in an early autobiographical novel, *My Argument with the Gestapo*:

> The thought of Cambridge takes fire, feverishly, in my mind, like the things that appeared to be cakes of solidified oatmeal they used for lighting fires in the slick grates of Clare New Court.
>
> The thought of you empties like old gin out of a glass that has been standing several days, among the clean plates.[12]

Claiming he has no knowledge of the world is perhaps part of his desire to transform himself. He has donned the persona of holiness, imposed by the Catholic world but consciously accepted by him. For a time, Merton indeed got caught up in his quick fame as the new and popular "expert" on Catholic spirituality. One wonders what his brother monks, many having spent *decades* at Gethsemani, thought of him, for he is merely a bit more than a neophyte, baptized fewer than ten years ago, and here he is now writing books on how to become a contemplative!

To his credit, he soon realizes the reality of this false Self, *his* false Self, a realization eventually to evolve into his own concept of the True Self. Masks, however, were always a part of his life (and admittedly, a part of ours, too!); not only did he use them in his several unpublished novels (most of his protagonists were Merton himself, and Michael Mott lists over fifty names behind which Merton hid), but he also brought them into the abbey.

The shadow hides behind masks (as well as in our projections). Jolande Jacobi says, "The confrontation with the shadow and its integration must always be achieved first in the individuation process in order to strengthen the ego for further laps in the journey and for the crucial encounter with the Self."[13]

While reading St. Bernard of Clairveaux, Merton first comes across the concept of the "false self." Merton writes:

> After all, what is your personal identity? It is what you really are, your real self. None of us is what he thinks he is, or what other people think he is, still less what his passport says he is....And it is fortunate for most of us that we are mistaken. We do not generally know what is good for us. That is because, in St. Bernard's language, our true personality has been concealed under the "disguise" of a false self, the ego whom we tend to worship in place of God.[14]

This idea corresponds to Jung's belief that in the first stages of individuation, the ego considers itself the center of the psyche rather than the archetypal Self (which for Western man is Christ). Jung says:

> Anyone who has any ego-consciousness at all takes it for granted that he knows himself. But the ego knows only its own contents, not the unconscious and its contents. People measure their self-knowledge by what the average person in their social environment knows of himself, but not by the real psychic facts which are for the most part hidden from them.[15]

The ego constructs a disguise, a *persona*, that obfuscates its relationship to the Self. This mask is also presented to the world; it is not a reflection of the Self, but quite the contrary; it is often a flattering mask that *pretends* to qualities the person does not possess. The more false the persona, the more ego-oriented the individual. Being so cleverly constructed, masks often fool people, as well as the wearer, but usually in a moment of unguardedness, the mask slips, revealing the wearer's true Self. It can be a humiliating moment for the person involved, realizing then how much of his or her life is based upon a lie. It can also be a freeing moment if one is open to it, for masks can be discarded.

An individuated person (one who is *integrated*), however, understands the true function of the persona: He wears his persona consciously, one that is true to his personality type. An individuated person knows that he is *not* the persona. He also understands the social necessity of a persona: a means of protecting one's vulnerability, at the same time allowing healthy interaction with other people.

In *Seeds of Contemplation*, Merton is preoccupied with the idea of false and True Self because in the early stages of his career as monk/writer, there was a tendency among his readers to canonize by acclamation the young monk. Merton is likely aware that he perhaps does not have the credentials—"the chops"—to present himself as an authority on contemplation, being a new convert and a novice in mysticism. He perhaps feels that he has donned a false mask. We can imagine his thinking, "If they only knew the *real* me." If he had been plagued by such thoughts (not being what he appeared to be) when he applied to the Franciscans, it is likely that he was still plagued by such thoughts at Gethsemani. In fact, a close reading of his journals proves that very early on in his life as a monk, he is haunted by the idea that he may be a "fake" contemplative. For the most part, he blames the Abbey of Gethsemani for his failure to become a true contemplative, thus his obsession with becoming a Carthusian (an order so austere and so rare that there is only *one* Carthusian monastery in the U.S.).

What complicates Merton's becoming his True Self is his pursuit of *perfection*. He writes, "The only true joy on earth is to escape from the prison of our own self-hood….Short of this perfection, created things do not bring us joy but pain."[16] True joy and peace, Jung says, comes not from *escape* but from the *embrace* of opposites, of the dark and the light residing in each one of us (elements of this are found in Zoroastrianism and Buddhism). Merton's divided psyche is clearly revealed in the following passage, a prayer illustrating his avoidance of facing his shadow:

> Therefore keep me, above all things, *from* sin. Keep me *from* the death of deadly sin which puts hell in my soul. Keep me *from* the murder of lust that blinds and poisons my heart. Keep me *from* the sins that eat a man's flesh with irresistible fire until he is devoured.[17]

His prayer could as easily be, "Lord, keep me from my shadow," a prayer that leads to frustration and lack of self-knowledge. But no matter what lengths individuals go to in order to ignore their shadow, it manifests itself either in projections or in dreams. Merton would have been wiser to *accept* his shadow, realize it, and embrace it. It would have provided the peace and freedom he so longed for.

We do not wish to belabor Merton's ongoing problem with his shadow, for even as he writes *Seeds of Contemplation*, he knows in his heart that true sanctity's sine qua non is love for all people: "I must look for my identity somehow, not only in God but in other men."[18] The word *somehow* is a poignant cri de coeur; Merton intellectually understands he must learn to love the world of men and women. Monastic life with its self-examination, prayer, fasting and privation, solitude and silence will gradually provide the necessary breakthrough to a healing of his wounded heart, but it will demand much soul-searching and soul work, even suffering. He performs the work required. Even at the end of his second journal, he feels he has accomplished a great deal in becoming his True Self; he writes, "I have become very different from what I used to be. The man who began this journal is dead." In Jungian terms, it is not so much death, but a stripping away of masks, allowing them to "die."[19]

# Chapter Five

A few months after his ordination, while saying Mass, Merton faints at the altar. He diagnoses himself, explaining it is the result of the medicine he has been taking for his stomach ailments. In fact, he is on the threshold of a nervous collapse, reminiscent of the time he almost fainted on the Long Island Railroad. In her biography of Merton, Monica Furlong observes, "It was ironic and wounding to repeat that collapse in a contemplative monastery."[1] He is, as usual, doing too much. The year 1949 alone sees the publication of three books (although one was written five years before). There is also his daily journaling, his voluminous reading, his faithfully following the Divine Office (after the Second Vatican Council, 1962–65, known as the Liturgy of the Hours), and the celebration of daily Mass—it all takes its toll on him.

He is hard on himself, overscrupulous about celebrating Mass, doubting whether or not he has said the words properly. He still joins in communal, manual labor, working along with the other monks in the hot Kentucky cornfields. He is stretching himself too thin. He is also still plagued by his shadow: "My soul was cringing and doubling up and subconsciously getting ready for the next tidal wave. At the moment all I had left in my heart was an abyss of self-hatred—waiting for the next appalling sea."[2]

There is no doubt that by the end of 1949 Merton is depressed, if not clinically, then at least in body, mind, and spirit. "Tomorrow it will be eight years since I came to Gethsemani. I somehow feel less clean than I did then when I thought I was throwing my civil identity away."[3] His entry reveals that he is incapable of being compassionate toward himself. This is not to say he was a man *always* gloomy and unhappy, for he is not; but he remains a man yet to achieve self-acceptance or world acceptance, the world for which he prays every day of his life. He is also a new priest who has just lost his father figure with the death of his abbot, Frederick Dunne in 1948, the man who placed the published *The Seven Storey Mountain* into Merton's hands, the man who encouraged Merton to write a book that would inspire people to love and pursue the spiritual life.

He enjoys working in the woods, but even there he is overwhelmed: "I felt lonely and small and humiliated—chopping down dead trees with a feeling that perhaps I was not even a real person any more."[4] Plagued by such feelings of fear, dejection, and unworthiness, he believes the cure for his problems is *more* solitude. At this time, Merton is reading Rainer Maria Rilke, the poet par excellence of solitude. (As early as February 1, 1947, Merton was dreaming of a hermitage: "I agree that one hermitage for one hermit stands a good chance of being beautiful!")[5]

In a rather long journal entry for December 20, 1949, Merton finally admits to being a contemplative near collapse from overwork: he is breathing hard, his heartbeat is fast, and he has developed a dry cough. There is also a detailed description of a manic drive he took with the abbey jeep, skidding in and out of ditches and ending up sideways in the middle of a road with a car heading straight for him. He somehow returns the jeep to the monastery, covered from head to foot with mud.

No doubt about it, he is a man in trouble on many fronts.

The year 1950 starts out peaceably. The first English edition of *Selected Poems* appears as well as his book *What Are These Wounds?* It is the year he ended up in the hospital in Louisville with colitis. He also had a chest X-ray and a nose operation. While in the hospital, he vomits blood that has accumulated in his stomach. His doctor recommends a long rest, which Merton summarily dismisses, joking that it is the doctor who needs a vacation.

By the end of 1950, Merton has been nine years at Gethsemani. He summarizes his health by saying that his guts are broken, and he is required to take liver shots with a long needle.

In 1951, Abbot Fox appointed Merton as the master of scholastics (1951–55). Merton assumes the assignment seriously, gazing deeply into the eyes of his young men and willingly taking up "their burdens upon me."[6] The abbot wisely realizes that Merton, with probable psychosomatic illnesses, needs to shift his gaze from himself to something outside himself; therefore, Merton would benefit from being master of scholastics, as would the scholastics under his charge, directed by the most gifted monk in Gethsemani.

Merton himself understands his psychosomatic tendencies: "Today a headache and upset stomach, which are probably psychosomatic or perhaps come from too many useless medicines."[7] It is during his time as master of scholastics that Merton is forbidden by the abbot to maintain a journal; there are no journal entries from March 10, 1953, to July 17, 1956.

Prior to the order to cease with his journals, Merton is still obsessed with his need for greater solitude, a preoccupation that consumes him to the point that he speaks to a psychiatrist friend of his, Dr. Philip Law, who advises Merton in 1952 to leave Gethsemani and start his *own* contemplative order. His advice is surely music to Merton's ears, but it is not that easy. Merton has taken a vow of *stability* and would need a dispensation, which means his request would have to pass through the labyrinthine Trappist bureaucracy (and possibly the Vatican). It is unlikely that the Trappists would give up Merton without a fight.

Dom Gabriel Sortais (1902–63), abbot of Bellefontaine, is elected abbot general of the Order of Cistercians of the Strict Observance (OCSO), or Trappists, in 1951, following the resignation of Dom Dominique Nogues. Merton already knows Dom Sortais from his visits to Gethsemani as vicar general, having served as his interpreter. When Sortais becomes abbot general, Merton begins a correspondence with him about his writing, censorship, and particularly his stability difficulties. Merton is still enamored of the Carthusians, but there are other possibilities for transfer: Camaldoli (yet another reform of the Benedictines), a South American foundation, the West Indies, and Cuernavaca, Mexico. Dom Humphrey writes to invite Merton to Sky Farm in Vermont, the first American Charterhouse (the English term for a Carthusian monastery).

Since we have no journals for the years 1953–55, Merton's letters to Dom Sortais are invaluable, revealing both Merton's mental and spiritual state. His comments are intriguing, sometimes quite candid, other times coy, sometimes accusatory, sometimes humble, sometimes proud, and at other times cunning.

Merton's first letters to Abbot General Sortais contain his candid opinion about his abbot's journey to Utah to begin another foundation, to which Merton is opposed. But if there *is* to be a foundation, Merton's idea is to send half of their students in theology, a suggestion Merton begs Sortais not to mention to his abbot.[8]

Merton also wrote about his book *The Sign of Jonas* (1953). Sortais opposes its publication (on the advice of censors), upsetting Merton, but he is ever the obedient monk: "The wound you give me, dear Most Reverend Father, is salutary and merciful."[9] He also again expresses his desire to be a saint but feels he may only be good enough to be thrown to a whale, *The Sign of Jonas* very much on his mind.

He confesses to Sortais his state of soul: "I am scared by the nothingness that opens like an abyss to my soul." He admits to discussing with his abbot his desire for more solitude, and that he need not seek the desert, for "the desert is myself."[10] Sortais was likely surprised by such revelations of the heart, and he must have been moved by the following Merton letter of March 13, 1953:

> The question of the journal is very simple. You ask me if this task is not bound to hinder my intimate relations with God. Well, if it were God's will that I do this task, He would Himself see to it how to protect me. As I wrote in *The Sign of Jonas*, I felt clearly I was doing His holy will and, though I had a few distractions, I think my interior life did not suffer too much. But now you are showing your wish to see the journal cease. Since this does not please you, I willingly discard the work, which kept me busy only very little as a matter of fact. It is no longer God's will that I write this journal. Of course my relations with Him would be hindered. There we are. I find the answer is very simple.
>
> 1. Is it your will that I don't write *any more a single* book?
> 2.  Or do you want me not to write a book while I am Student Master?
> 3. Do you allow the eventual publication of the conferences given to the students, and of the main ideas of their formation?
> 4. Or, apart from the journal and every autobiographical and formally "personal" narrative, would you allow a book, provided it does not hinder the interior life and does not disagree with our monastic ideal—e.g., meditations, studies on the interior life, lives of saints, studies in Holy Scripture, etc.?[11]

Merton also pleads his case for more solitude: "I am more convinced than ever of the necessity of a truly solitary, truly contemplative life, and I am just as fully convinced I will never achieve it by making complicated projects."[12] In another letter, he complains about being near despair, but Merton bounces back, later informing Sortais that he spent a good Lent and that he has gained insights into himself, his major "sin" being his lack of humility.[13] He also assures Sortais that he has not given up on his desire to become a saint.

He continues to write Sortais about solitude, but at one point he seemingly has settled the problem: "It is not my solitude I seek, but His solitude. And that solitude, I begin to see, is quite incomprehensible."[14] But the question is far from settled. Merton does not give up on his desire for more solitude and soon begins his quest to become a hermit.

In a letter to Dom Jean Leclerq, he writes that he has stopped writing (not quite the whole truth) and would renounce it for good if he could live in solitude. But he knows that it is likely impossible for him to give writing up forever: "Writing is deep in my nature, and I cannot deceive myself that it will be very easy for me to do without it."[15]

Not writing continues to take its toll on Merton. In a letter to Abbot James Fox, he describes his mental state: "On the whole, my nerves are not too good and I can't rely on my faculties as I used to—they play tricks on me, and I get into nervous depression and weakness....But I hope it is the darkness before the dawn."[16] In another letter to Fox, he sounds even more desperate: "I beg Him to give me grace to carry this [God's will] through in spite of darkness, depression and disgust. I know I yet have to grow very much in the spirit of faith—and need much more hope."[17]

It is during this time that Merton's interest in and study of psychology burgeons. He believes that knowledge of psychology would help him with his own problems. He also believes that it would render him a better, more astute master of scholastics, many of whom are having trouble adjusting to monastic life, exhibiting both mental and physical symptoms. He also concludes that the abbey should do a better job in screening candidates psychologically, quickly rooting out any neurotic applicants. His reading *Notebook Nine, Ad Usum* lists the subjects he is studying:

- 1955 CONFLICT
- 1955 FREUD, S.
- 1955 GANDHI, M
- 1955 JUNG, C.G.
- 1955 NARCISSISM
- 1955 NEURO-PSYCH THEORY
- 1955 NIEBUHR, R
- 1955 NON - VIOLENCE (GANDHI)
- 1955 NORMAL PERSONALITY
- 1955 PIUS XII (& PSYCHOTHERAPY)
- 1955 PSYCHIATRIC DISORDERS
- 1955 PSYCHOANALYSIS TODAY
- 1955 PSYCHOANALYTIC THEORY OF NEUROSIS
- 1955 PSYCHOLOGY
- 1955 PSYCHOTHERAPY (PIUS XII)
- 1955 THERAPY[18]

It is not surprising that Merton felt the need to delve into a study of psychology to help him understand his scholastics (and himself), just as Carl Jung felt no trepidation about entering theological waters with his essay "Psychoanalysis and the Cure of Souls." Jung admits to having more success in cures of Catholics than Protestants because of the Catholic sacrament of Penance. He understands, however, the precarious nature of juxtaposing religion and psychology and writes, "The question of the relations between psychoanalysis and the pastoral cure of souls is not easy to answer, because the two are concerned with essentially different things. The cure of souls as practiced by the clergyman or priest is a religious influence based on a Christian confession of faith. Psychoanalysis, on the other hand, is a medical intervention, a psychological technique whose purpose it is to lay bare the contents of the unconscious and integrate them into the conscious mind."[19]

Merton, as revealed by his reading notebook, is intent on understanding psychoanalysis, and he also believes he can successfully practice it as master of scholastics. His motive is pure, but he surely has no business posing even as an amateur psychologist. He writes to his agent Naomi Burton that he wants to learn to give Rorschach tests. He has taken the test himself, and is surprised to be informed that he is not a solitary but social person! He also begins giving the tests to his scholastics. He admits to botching the reading of one Rorschach test by misinterpreting it. The young man, he concludes, is trying to be the kind of man and monk he thinks Merton wants him to be. Merton is very contrite about how incompetently he advised the young man, likely complicating his monastic adjustment problems.[20]

In the 1950s, however, psychiatry is in the air, and many believe it is *the* answer to soul/psyche problems. Merton is not immune to this, and neither is Abbot James Fox. He knows Merton is experiencing depression, insomnia, stomach ailments, feelings of failure; he also knows that Merton has written an article, "Neurosis in the Monastic Life," and that copies of it have been sent to a number of people, including the well-known psychiatrist Gregory Zilboorg of New York City.

Like Merton, Zilboorg is a convert to Catholicism. He is a Russian Jew born in 1890 and was trained as a doctor and psychiatrist. When he set up his practice in America, he served as psychoanalyst to fashionable and famous people, including

Ernest Hemingway, George Gershwin, and Moss Hart. Merton wants to meet him to discuss his article; however, Dom James Fox is not about to let Merton loose in New York City. But when he learns that Zilboorg is scheduled to lecture at St. John's University in Collegeville, Minnesota, he allows Merton along with Father John Eudes (a doctor who became a psychiatrist—and later an abbot and then a hermit) to attend the conference.

Merton's journal entry for July 29, 1956, (in volume three, *A Search for Solitude*, there are no journal entries between March 11, 1953, and July 16, 1956) is revelatory, both psychologically and spiritually:

> A great loneliness is necessary, a loneliness and a detachment that nothing can comfort and no one can satisfy. Probably one of the most painful elements is the fear and indeed the risk, of illusion.
>
> In this loneliness and peril one must move forward with inexorable desire. A desire that will finally take one over the precipice, into the fullness of peace—the leap into pure faith, pure prayer.
>
> …On a deeper level, desire and conflict. In the greatest depths, like a spring of pure water rising up in the flames of hell, is the smallness, the frailty of a hope that is, yet, never overwhelmed but continues strangely and inexplicably to nourish in the midst of apparent despair.[21]

Such an eloquent passage is illustrative as to why Merton speaks to so many people who are struggling with depression or who are in despair. Often overwhelmed by his own psychological problems, he keeps the flame of hope alive, and when we try to analyze why it never is extinguished, we come up with one reason: Merton never for a day gives up on prayer.

Just after this passage, Merton writes about Zilboorg, who has informed Merton that his article "Neurosis in Monastic Life" is too hastily written and if published would do more harm than good. He suggests that Merton permanently shelve the article (it was reworked and published posthumously in the *Merton Annual* IV, 1991).

Later, he has a one-on-one talk with Zilboorg, who informs Merton that he is neurotic, "very stubborn," "afraid to be an ordinary monk," wanting "to be famous…a big shot," and finally a narcissist. He also describes Merton's desire to be a hermit as "pathological."[22] These are harsh things to say, but to his credit Merton records them, and on the day afterwards, he writes to his agent Naomi Burton Stone, saying that "Zilboorg has been terrific."[23] He informs her that Zilboorg's lectures are also "terrific." The whole experience at St. John's, he said, has gone well.

Is Merton being completely honest? Surely some of Zilboorg's remarks were brusque, if not wounding, but for the most part, Merton *accepts* Zilboorg's assessment of his personality. Zilboorg is a brash man, however, full of high sentence and ego, and does not tolerate being contradicted. If Merton is a star in the publishing world, Zilboorg is a star in his world of psychiatry, sought after by celebrities, by radio, and by television. But he then ventures too far. During the second week of the conference, Dom Fox arrives. Merton has a second meeting with Dom Fox present. Zilboorg in front of the abbot analyzes Merton, rather indelicately and, some consider, cruelly, repeating, "You want a hermitage in Times Square with a large sign over it saying 'Hermit'."

Totally humiliated, Merton silently sits with tears streaming down his face, muttering, "Stalin! Stalin!"[24] It is a painful narrative to read. Had Zilboorg himself harbored animosity or jealousy towards Merton? Were his comments his own psychological projections?

Merton passively accepts the criticism, but in a journal entry several years later (Zilboorg died in 1959), he writes, "I thought today at adoration what a blessing it was that I did not go in 1956 to be analyzed by Zilboorg! What a tragedy and mess that would have been—and I must give Z. the credit for having sensed it himself in his own way. It would have been utterly impossible and absurd....He had quite enough intelligence to see that it would be a very poor production for him, for the abbot (who was most willing) and for me. I am afraid that I was willing, at the same time, to go, which shows what a fool I was."[25]

Psychoanalysis may have indeed helped Merton through some of his difficulties, but Merton in hindsight wisely realizes that Zilboorg was not the analyst for him.

We question what role, if any, Abbot Fox played in this situation. We know he did not want Merton to leave Gethsemani, and he may (or may not) have used Zilboorg's comments to discourage a dispensation of Merton's vow of stability. Zilboorg later visited Merton at Gethsemani, and Merton records the visit as an affable one with Zilboorg kinder in his tone with gentle reminders for Merton to just calm down. Quite the opposite of his last encounter, but the damage had already been done—*and* in front of the abbot. Were Zilboorg's comments ever used against Merton, that is, to keep him from transferring from Gethsemani?

Before leaving this period of Merton's life, we should take a closer look at the now infamous article Zilboorg so brutally attacked. Was it such a bad article? Merton reworked it, and it is now available to be read. If anything, it is a reliable account of Merton's hard-won attempts to understand his own psychological problems; in other words, the article is nearly a self-confession of Merton's psychic state. Consider the following:

> Anxiety is not always felt. Sometimes, beneath the apparently calm surface of the soul, there is severe

anxiety at work, but the subject is not conscious of it. This anxiety may leave its mark not on his soul but on his physical organism. It may be taking effect in a stomach ulcer, colitis, or other psychosomatic sicknesses. It may register as palpitation of the heart, pain in the cardiac area, or other things which the patient interprets as signs of sickness. In such cases, anxiety is objectified as a physical sickness, real or imaginary.[26]

Zilboorg could not have found fault with the above passage as it is psychologically insightful and balanced. But more important it is a valid psychological description of Merton at the time. He was, indeed, plagued by psychosomatic illnesses, the result of his many conflicts, particularly those with the abbot over his desire for more solitude.

In early 1953, Dom Fox threw Merton a bone—or extends an olive branch: He allows Merton to use an old toolshed that has been hauled by the Traxcavator to the woods beyond the horse pasture; for a time, Merton spends hours there alone—his first "hermitage." Merton is thrilled with the abbot's concession: It is a place where he has no distractions and everything is serene and the view beautiful.

# Chapter Six

Carl Jung believed men and women are psychologically androgynous. He designates a man's feminine component as the *anima* and a woman's masculine component as the *animus*. Psychological growth for a man and a woman demands the assistance of the contra-sexual archetype. The specific function of a man's anima is to serve as a mediatrix between the ego, the center of the conscious mind, and the Self, which is the center of the unconscious as well as the regulating force of the total psyche. When a man listens to his anima, he is led into the deepest regions of the unconscious where the source of wisdom and self-knowledge abides. The anima also assists a man in discovering the personal symbols that will release Eros, the principle of relatedness without which he cannot connect either with the Self or people in the external world. The anima, likewise, provides the libido, energy necessary for the further development of the personality. Jungian analyst John Sanford writes:

> When the anima functions in her correct place, she serves to broaden and enlarge a man's consciousness, and to enrich his personality by infusing into him, through dreams, fantasies, and inspired ideas, an awareness of an inner world of psychic images and life-giving emotions. A man's consciousness tends to be too constricted, and without contact with the unconscious, becomes dry and sterile.[1]

Since it is through dreams that the anima most often appears, interpretation of dreams is the cornerstone of Jung's analytic method. Jung recorded and interpreted many of his dreams in his autobiography, *Memories, Dreams, Reflections*. He viewed dreams as "utterances of the unconscious," the primary means through which the unconscious communicates with the conscious mind. Dreams, therefore, are symbolic letters that, if decoded wisely, reveal much about one's personality, about one's psychological/spiritual problems. In his own encounter with his anima, Jung records the following:

> Then a new idea came to me in putting down all this material for analysis. I was in effect writing letters to the anima, that is, to a part of myself with a different viewpoint from my conscious one.[2]

He later says about the anima:

> It is she who communicates the images of the unconscious to the conscious mind, and that is what I chiefly valued her for. For decades I always turned to the anima when I felt that my emotional behavior was disturbed.[3]

Merton, too, recorded many of his dreams both in his published and unpublished journals. He obviously believed that they were an important part of his inner life and that an understanding of his dreams increased self-knowledge. Many of his dreams concern his anima. The precursor of his famous "Proverb-dream" occurred in May of 1957:

> In a dream—people dancing—new dances and great gestures, like the Russian ballet. One of the dancers in

a tight-fitting velvet of a beautiful leaf green, was a dark-haired woman with her hair cut close like a boy's. In the middle of the dance she bent over sideways and touched the floor with both hands in a curious gesture. I observed that the people dancing were elegant and serious and bored and the expressions of boredom were slightly different from what they used to be when I was in the world.[4]

Before Merton became engrossed in Boris Pasternak's writing and his subsequent winning of the Nobel Prize in 1958, Merton had been reading Nikolai Berdyaev, a radical Russian Christian he had come to admire. Thus his Russian dream is not a surprise, reflecting Merton's interest in Russian mysticism. The dance imagery suggests that Berdyaev has influenced Merton's thinking, for it was he who stated that sin is inertia (aka sloth or acedia—one of the seven deadly sins). Dance is the antithesis of inertia: It is graceful, beautiful movement. A soul in grace is also beautiful. The dancer's touching the ground is symbolic of humankind's purpose in the world: to be grounded in the world and to live (dance) beautifully. The dancer's touching the floor also symbolizes Merton's way of touching the world: *through his writing*. The only negative aspect of the dream is the dancers' faces: They appear almost like automatons. This may be a reflection of Merton's feelings: He is the "guilty bystander" divorced from the world because he often did not perceive himself involved in the dance of life but removed from it by his own will.

It was at this time that Merton seriously questioned his role in the world. The dream also occurred after the mortifying Zilboorg affair and after Merton's six months of not writing in his journal. To deny himself journaling is to deny his impulse to write, which is his way to "dance"—his way to touch. Although he often complained about his writing, Merton would surely be bored, like the audience, if he could never write again. But he wants his writing not to be escapist but to address the world's issues, to concern the East and the West and ways to bring them together, including the country with which America was having a cold war: Russia. (Whereas ennui appears on the dancers' faces, it is significant to note that nearly a year later Merton's outlook dramatically changes, seeing love and Proverb on the faces of the people in the Louisville Vision.)

❧

On February 28, 1958, Merton dreamed the following:

> On a porch at Douglaston I am embraced with deter-
> mined and virginal passion by a young, Jewish girl.
> She clings to me and will not let me go, and I get to
> like the idea. I see that she is a nice kid in a plain, sin-
> cere sort of way. I reflect, "She belongs to the same
> race as St. Anne." I ask her name and she says her
> name is Proverb. I tell her that is a beautiful name and
> significant name, but she does not appear to like it—
> perhaps others have mocked her for it.[5]

The dream ego, Merton (at his current age), and the Jewish girl (much younger and symbolizing the Eternal Feminine) meet on the porch of his grandparents' home. The porch, symbol of receptivity (in early American life the traditional locus of girl-boy encounters), is a threshold or an entrance into the house. The house symbolizes the psyche. The girl represents Merton's anima. When she embraces him with "virginal passion," they are unified: one man/woman. Thus, the embrace is symbolic of *coni-unctio*, which Jung defines as the inner marriage. True to the Logos impulse in all men, Merton asks her name. She gives a symbolic name, "Proverb." A proverb is a maxim, a wise saying;

hence, Proverb is a spiritual guide, a wisdom figure leading Merton into the house of the psyche where wisdom awaits.

Merton deduces that Proverb is "mocked by others" (consider his "refusal of woman"). These "others" are elements of Merton's own personality, which disparage the feminine in favor of the rational, intellectual, masculine way of the world. The Jews, the stewards of holy wisdom from time immemorial, have often been mocked, being of "the same race as St. Anne," the mother of Mary, the mother of God.

A close reading (if, perhaps, overly determined) of the dream also suggests noteworthy biographical information about Merton. Merton's father and mother were married in St. Anne's Church in Soho, London. He named his first hermitage, an old abandoned toolshed at Gethsemani, after St. Anne. And as a young man attending school in England, Merton met his friend Andrew Winser's sister Ann, who made a lifelong impression on him. In 1965, after thirty years since they first met, Merton writes:

> I suddenly thought of Ann Winser, Andrew's little sister. She was about twelve or thirteen....A dark and secret child. One does not fall in love with a child of thirteen and I hardly remember even thinking of her or noticing her, yet the other day I realized that I had never forgotten her and that she had made a deep impression.[6]

When Merton lived with his grandparents in Douglaston, he often used the porch as a place to read the Bible and to sleep. That sleep would be associated with the Douglaston porch, along with reading the Bible (perhaps the Book of Proverbs), and Merton's sense of shame—he was afraid to be caught reading the

Bible—adds to the significance of his dream, one resonating with hints about Merton's life and personality.

To enter more deeply into the meaning of his dream, Merton initiates a dialogue with Proverb through a series of love letters. Jung would laud Merton's active engagement with his anima; it is a form of Active Imagination, a method of communing with unconscious elements in order to elicit their full import. In these letters, Merton thanks Proverb for appearing to him in his dreams and for awakening in him things that he thought he had lost forever.

In a letter to Proverb dated March 4, 1958, Merton notes that the great difference in their ages does not matter and writes:

> Dearest Proverb, I love your name, its mystery, its simplicity and its secret, which even you yourself seem not to appreciate.[7]

Merton's description of his anima along with its nomenclature correlates in remarkable similarity with Jung's own diction about *his* anima:

> Something strangely meaningful clings to her…a secret knowledge or hidden wisdom…in her lies something like a hidden purpose which seems to reflect a superior knowledge of life's laws.[8]

What exactly did Merton think he had *lost*? Perhaps the severity of his mother who wrote him a letter to inform him of her impending death frightened him to the point that he could never completely trust a woman again. He certainly lost the opportunity to experience a real, heartfelt good-bye with his mother. He himself wrote that "perhaps solitaries are made by severe mothers."[9]

And perhaps in his flight from the world and its perceived evils into Gethsemani, Merton became too self-absorbed, too focused on his own inner journey that he failed to concern himself about his brothers and sisters struggling to save their souls in the labyrinthine ways of the world. Maybe Merton just realized that in encountering Proverb, he owed much to the women he knew; there were many who enriched his life, women like his grandmother, Aunt Maud, Catherine de Hueck Doherty, Ginny Burton, his agent Naomi Burton Stone, and let us not forget his many girlfriends, even the girl with whom he fathered a child. Now as an older man, he is writing letters to his own "inner woman." The embrace of the dream anima is, then, the beginning of a breakthrough in Merton's individuation: It symbolically portrays Merton's willingness to accept the feminine, an acceptance that Jung calls the "masterpiece"[10] of the individuation process. Keep in mind, however, that the anima initiates the embrace of Merton; she is "determined," and she "clings" to Merton; she is demanding recognition because as her youth suggests, she is an undeveloped aspect of Merton's personality.

On March 19, 1958, Merton experienced his famous "Louisville Vision," recalled in his journal:

> Yesterday, in Louisville, at the corner of 4th and Walnut, suddenly I realized that I loved all the people and that none of them were or could be totally alien to me. As if waking from a dream—the dream of my separateness, of the "special" vocation to be different. My vocation does not really make me different from the rest of men or put me in a special category except artificially, juridically. I am still a member of the human race—and what more glorious destiny is there for man, since the Word was made flesh and became, too, a member of the human race.[11]

In a letter dated October 23, 1958, Merton describes this event to the Russian writer Boris Pasternak. Merton writes:

> . I was walking alone in the crowded street and sud-
> denly saw that everybody was Proverb and that in all of
> them shone her extraordinary beauty and purity and
> shyness, even though they did not know who they
> were and were perhaps ashamed of their names—
> because they were mocked on account of them. And
> they did not know their real identity as the Child so
> dear to God who, from before the beginning, was lay-
> ing in His sight all days, playing in the world.[12]

This is definitely not the Merton who entered Gethsemani fraught with contempt of the world. Nor is he the Merton who, eleven years before in the Cincinnati airport, thought that the passersby were infected with corruption brought in by planes from New York. This is a new Merton, one able to embrace the human race, an act made possible by his anima, Proverb. As a man is *physically* born of a woman, so is he *spiritually* and *psychologically* reborn through and by a woman: Merton's inner woman, Proverb.

Not long after his Proverb dream and the Louisville Vision, Merton visited his artist friend Victor Hammer. He was emotionally attracted to a painting depicting a young woman offering a crown to a young man. He questioned Hammer about the woman's identity (just as he questioned Proverb). Hammer was uncertain, explaining that the male figure was Christ, but the identity of the woman was questionable; it could be Mary or another woman. Mystified, Merton perused the features of the young maiden.

After his viewing of the painting, Merton wrote to Mr. Hammer:

The feminine principle in the universe is the inexhaustible source of creative realization of the Father's glory in the world and is in fact the manifestation of His glory.[13]

The above sentence is the origin of one of Merton's most famous and haunting prose poems, "Hagia Sophia." Proverb had graced Merton with the Louisville Vision; she also inspired him to write this beautiful poem. When a man connects with his anima (his muse), his creativity is activated. "Hagia Sophia" is a poem worthy of close reading, not only because of its haunting beauty but also because it charts Merton's journey from his previous "refusal of women" to his *acceptance* of the feminine principle in his life. That is not to say that, with the Proverb dreams and letters and "Hagia Sophia," the journey is complete. Far from it! Merton still has soul work to accomplish with the anima archetype, but he is at least well embarked upon the journey toward his anima integration.

🔹

On July 2, 1960, feast of the Visitation, at St. Anthony's Hospital, Merton records the following dream:

At 5:30, as I was dreaming in a very quiet hospital, the soft voice of the nurse awoke me gently from my dream—it was like awakening for the first time from all the dreams of my life——as if the Blessed Virgin herself, as if Wisdom had awakened me. We do not hear the soft voice, the gentle voice, the feminine voice, the voice of the Mother: yet she speaks everywhere and in everything. Wisdom cries out to the marketplace—"if anyone is little let him come to me." Who is more little than the helpless man, asleep in bed, having entrusted himself gladly to sleep and to night?

Him the gentle voice will awaken, all that is sweet in woman will awaken him. Not for conquest and pleasure, but for the far deeper wisdom of love and joy and communion.[14]

This dream is numinous. Merton is awakened, and not just by anyone but by the Feminine, here represented by the Blessed Virgin herself who is also feminine Wisdom, both of whom symbolize Merton's anima. His anima figure is speaking to him. He knows that in the past, he has not listened to the "soft voice, the gentle, feminine voice." In fact, he has admitted to refusing to do so.

He wants to be "little" again, to be a child and to be tenderly cared for. Perhaps this wish is a lingering desire from childhood to be loved and cherished. Thus, the dream is linked to his relationship with his natural mother, who, he admits, was a "rather severe"[15] mother.

It is not an erotic dream: Merton seeks not pleasure or conquest from the feminine (of which he had plenty in his secular days) but the "far deeper wisdom of love and joy and communion."[16]

❦

On September 7, 1962, the vigil of Our Lady's Nativity, Merton records this rather longish dream:

I am in a village "near Bardstown," out of the monastery, it is late, the monks are going to bed—will I get back to bedtime or be out after dark. It is dusk, still daylight.

With another man [Tony Walsh?] we meet two lovely young women dressed in white, in the almost deserted village. I say delightedly, "With you, we will easily get a ride!" We plan to hitchhike, so as to get back to the monastery before it is too late.

They smile and do not object. I pair off with the less nunlike of the two (the other has a suggestion of a hood or veil) and with my arm around her waist, we walk off down the road. All through the dream I walk with my arm around her. She is fresh and firm and pure, a beautiful sweet person, a stranger yet freely intimate and loving. However, at one point she tells me seriously I must never need try to kiss her or to seduce her, and I assure her earnestly and sincerely I have no such intention. This does nothing to alter the intimacy of our relationship and friendship.

Hereafter the other two vanish out of the dream. I am with A. (Let us call her that, the question of knowing her *name* never really arises at all. It is totally irrelevant.)

Though the village has been dark and empty, now we are outside on the highway, at a crossroads. It is light. We decide that if possible we will take a bus to Bardstown and get from there to Gethsemani. Now there are half a dozen people waiting for the bus. They all know A. because she has preached in their village a new doctrine—(sort of Shaker theology)—and they twit her about it. One who kids her is an American Indian. Another says something with lewd implications and I solemnly and hotly defend her— she lets me know it is hardly necessary.

The bus comes, I get in the front, there is nobody there. A. comes in through another door. We meet in the bus.

We are out of the bus, again in the midst of the country.

I see a chapel. It is the chapel of a novitiate of a foundation of Gethsemani, Genesee (Je ne sais pas!) [I do not know]. We will go to the monastery and wake them up. They will understand, someone will give us a ride.

Outside the monastery, a young secular and two or three girls. They are in bathing suits, have been swimming in a pond in the farmyard. We will not wake up the monks. This boy will drive us. But we must get to his car without awaking anyone.

Complication in the build-up. We do not find the car.

On the road. High columns of silver grey smoke go up from the direction of Bardstown. "Tactical atomic weapons." Beautiful though. Some kind of test. It is here I think A. told me not to kiss her.

We turn back. Now all the monks led by their abbot, Dom Eusebius, are out on the road, dressed as soldiers! He leads them with determination, surely I will be caught. As we pass through the midst of them A. conceals my monastic crown with her hand. But is this going to be enough?

Are they after us?

I am in a barn (without A.). I set fire to straw—if the barn burns it will divert any pursuit. But can I myself get out? After seeming to be trapped, I am now completely out, on the "other side" in open country, see a vast landscape, most moving with a church in the middle, Dutch with a thin spire—and sacred objects in the sky or country around, for instance a cross.

I am going past the church with the open country when I wake up.[17]

Dreams reflect our inner longings as well as our outer, conscious life. What was then on Merton's mind? Well, he had recently met with Tony Walsh from Montreal. He also had been thinking of Jim Forrest and the peace movement. He was seriously concerned about arms proliferation, fearing that not just war but "war" was on the horizon. Let us consider these facts as we try to understand this rather enigmatic dream.

The salient aspect of this dream is that it occurs *outside* the cloister of Gethsemani. Merton has admitted to his refusal of woman, but we must take into consideration that the Abbey of Gethsemani also refuses women, none of whom are allowed beyond its cloistered walls. Thus, for Merton to meet women, he must be *away* from the abbey, and we find him in a village near Bardstown where he meets two women. One he is attracted to because she does not look like the other, who reminds him of a nun. He thinks they will be better able to get a ride with a woman along (one thinks of Merton's love of movies, and he may be thinking of the movie *It Happened One Night*, with Clark Gable and Claudette Colbert, the latter, to Gable's astonishment, successfully hitching her shirt to win a ride).

Merton has his arm around the woman he names A. Why not give her a name? One reason may be that she represents the Eternal Feminine. The A. could represent the name of Anne, a sentimental name to Merton. It could also simply stand for the beginning of the alphabet, the genesis of language. But the name does not matter because Merton feels comfortable and at ease with A. She warns him that there is to be no kissing. This relationship is to be chaste. Merton assures A. that he does not intend to kiss her. He is a monk outside his monastery; therefore, he is breaking a rule.[18] But he will not break a more serious rule—his vow of chastity.

A bus drops them off at a chapel of the novitiate at Our Lady of the Genesee Abbey in Piffard, New York (near Buffalo). He sees more anima figures in the form of girls in bathing suits, so here we have hints of the erotic, but he is more afraid of waking up the monks, and needs a car for a getaway.

Suddenly he is back on the road and sees "silver grey smoke" in the air above Bardstown. He thinks, "tactical atomic weapons"—atomic war a constant preoccupation in his conscious life. He sees all of the Gethsemani monks are dressed as soldiers, and he wonders if they are "after us," that is, A. and him.

Is this what can happen to some men who go without contact with the feminine? Do they use atomic weapons? Do they become soldiers? And then the lovely gesture of A. as she covers his tonsure to protect him from being discovered: A. as his protector.

But having saved him, she suddenly disappears. He finds himself in a barn. The dream ego sets the straw on fire in order to make a diversion. He fears for his safety; he is now without A. to help him. He fears that he is trapped, but he suddenly finds himself on "the other side," the country—a new, open, vast country.

The burning of the barn is a reminder of Merton's fine poem "Elegy for the Monastery Barn." Fire also often suggests purgation. Why exactly does the dream ego burn down the barn? Is it to prevent himself from being caught by the soldier monks? Is he rejecting the old regime? Is he embracing the new ecumenism, now currently spreading throughout the church in the early 1960s? For renewal to occur, must there be a conflagration? It is through the fires of purgation, however, that the dream ego finds himself in a more beautiful landscape, a new "heaven and earth" with a church at its center. It appears that A. has led him to a better place, a holy place, whose Dutch church's spire (he had been reading Hans Küng's *The Council, Reform and Reunion*) is thin, reaching for the sky crowded with other "sacred objects," in particular a cross.

The dream ends: "I am going past the church with the open country when I wake up." He does not enter the church but walks by it. But why? Ambivalence? Disapproval? Does the "thin spire" suggest something negative? In other words, has the church with its changes "thinned" itself? We know Merton was unhappy about the loss of the Latin Mass and Gregorian chant, after the Second Vatican Council (1962–65), both of which he considered masterpieces.

Or is he passing the church to take the ecumenical Second Vatican Council (aka Vatican II) at its word, to explore other religions and their affinities with Catholicism?

❧

Another pivotal dream occurs on March 10, 1964:

Last night I dreamed that a distinguished Lady Latinist came to give a talk to the novices on St. Bernard. Instead of a lecture, she sang in Latin meters, flexes and puncta....The novices were restive and giggled. This made me sad. In the middle of the performance the late abbot Dom Frederic, solemnly entered. We all stood. The singing was interrupted. "Where did she come from," he asked. "Harvard," I said. Then the novices were all on a big semi, loaded on the elevator. I don't know how to go down from the top of the building. Instead of the Latinist coming on the elevator, I left the novices and escorted her down safely by the stairs, but now her clothes were all soiled and torn. She was confused and sad. She had no Latin and nothing much to say. I wonder what this dream is about. Is it about the Church? Is it about the liturgical revival, Anglicanism perhaps? Is it about some secret Anglican anima of my own?[19]

The Lady Latinist can certainly be construed as the Catholic Church ("Holy Mother Church"). She represents the church *before* Vatican II; therefore, she is the rejected former church whose language is now considered archaic (if not laughable), causing the novices to giggle. Merton is saddened by their reaction. He always loved the Latin language of the church; in fact, he never gave up reading his Latin breviaries, which he brought with him on his trip to Asia. He also wrote to Dom Ignace Gillet, "People are pushed into thinking that they are dissatisfied with the Latin, the Gregorian chant, the status of the lay brother, the liturgy as we have it, when in reality that is not the case at all....But it was only a few brothers who, moreover, were not always the best ones but who got more agitated and had more to say, and who tried to persuade the others to go with them, etc....But this is what I think about the Latin and the chant: They are masterpieces, which offer us an irreplaceable monastic and Christian experience."[20] The stairs symbolize the descent of the church, now soiled, worn, and in need of new clothes. The Lady is also confused and sad. The church of the sixties, whose endeavors to modernize and to update herself, confused and saddened many Catholics, including Merton. The Mass in the vernacular was, of course, the most controversial change for many in the church.

If by entering the Catholic Church and Gethsemani, Merton had replaced his mother and father with a new mother (church) and father (abbot, literally "father," from the Aramaic), then this dream is significant because it is reminiscent of his losing his mother. Keep in mind his mother was also a diarist, just like her son, so words were important to her. And now Latin is to be replaced by the vernacular. Merton (along with the millions of other Catholics) is anxious about it; he is losing something he values very much, and it is all tied up with the feminine, the anima. It is also quite clear that he is on the side of the Lady Latinist. This is a positive dream for Merton as it suggests that he is more and more moving toward an integration of his anima.

Generally, his dream reveals an ambiguity of response to the changing church of the sixties. The Lady Latinist represents the church Merton was received into on November 15, 1938, when he was baptized at Corpus Christi Church in New York. It was the Roman Catholic Church he loved so much: It was his new mother church, which perhaps saved him from a life of dissipation. Although Merton does not defend the Lady Latinist to Dom Frederick (now dead and replaced by Dom James Fox, a graduate of Harvard College, so Frederick Dunne may be said to represent the old church and James Fox the new church), he does not abandon her. Concerned for her safety, he escorts her down the stairs, the archaic means of descent, while the novices take the modern means of movement, the elevator, symbolic of the ecumenical movement. Implied in Merton's choice of the stairs over the elevator is perhaps a criticism that the church is changing—moving too quickly.

Dom Frederick Dunne is the male equivalent of the Lady Latinist. He represents the old order at Gethsemani, and had he lived (he died on August 4, 1948), he might have been disturbed by the changes of Vatican II. He was abbot of Gethsemani when Gregorian chant and the Latin Mass were the spiritual sustenance and treasure of Trappist monks. He was abbot before the basilica was stripped of its statues and its steeple removed. He was abbot when Merton entered Gethsemani, and he encouraged Merton to write his autobiography, *The Seven Storey Mountain*; he even handed to Merton the first published copy of his autobiography on July 7, 1948.

His successor was Dom James Fox, who led Gethsemani through the Vatican II period. He was also a graduate of Harvard Business School; he implemented sweeping changes at Gethsemani just as Vatican II would accomplish for the church at large. The old guard gave way to the new: the cycle of birth, death, and rebirth.

Although a positive dream, there is a negative side. Merton remains not completely comfortable with the feminine aspects of his personality. The cloister is symbolic of the psyche; there is *still* no place for the feminine within a cloister, which prohibits the presence of women. Furthermore, Merton himself does not comprehend her Latin singing; in other words, anima and the dream ego do not understand each other. He does not embrace her as he had embraced Proverb. He, at least, escorts her down the stairs and from the cloister, causing her clothes to become more soiled and torn. It suggests Merton, too, is guilty (soiled) and ambivalent (torn) about his anima, and by escorting her downstairs, symbolic of repression, he is avoiding her integration by relegating her to the unconscious, along with the male figures, representing his shadow.

In 1965, when writing in the journal later called *A Vow of Conversation*, Merton continued to refer to his "refusal of woman." On July 7, 1965, he wrote to Sister Mary Luke Tobin, recommending Karl Stern's new book, *The Flight from Woman*. He confessed that it was not so much that the nuns should take it to heart but that *he* should. He was conscious of his struggle to integrate the feminine into his life; consciousness of psychic imbalance facilitates its resolution.

❧

On November 19, 1964, Merton records the following dream:

Last night I had a haunting dream of a Chinese princess which stayed with me all day ("Proverb" again.) This lovely and familiar archetypal person. (No "object" yet how close and real, and how elusive!) She comes to me in various mysterious ways in my dreams. This time she

was with her "brothers" and I felt overwhelmingly the
freshness, the youth, the wonder, the truth of her; her
complete reality, more real than any other, yet, unobtainable. Yet I deeply felt the sense of her understanding, knowing and loving me, in my depths—not merely
in my individuality and everyday self, yet not as if this
self were utterly irrelevant to her. Not rejected, not
accepted either.[21]

The Chinese princess is an anima figure representing Merton's
interest in all things Eastern, including Chinese painting, Taoist
philosophy, and Zen Buddhism. The East is also (speaking broadly)
the land of compassion, the land of nothingness, the tea ceremony
and calligraphy, all of which fascinated Merton.

As early as 1962, Merton began corresponding with Dr.
John Wu, who helped Merton learn Chinese, culminating in one
of Merton's best books, *The Way of Chuang Tzu*, published in
1965. The journal *A Vow of Conversation* was also being written,
his most Zen-like journal. The poetic renditions of Chuang Tzu
were very much on Merton's mind at the time of his dream. John
Wu wrote to Merton on May 11, 1965, praising Merton's poems,
making Merton ecstatic. He wrote to Wu about how delighted he
was that he went ahead with the project. In June 1963, a year
prior to the dream, Merton had discovered his joy in reading
Chuang Tzu. Merton claimed it kept him sane.[22]

Because Merton's most numinous dreams of his anima
involve Proverb, it is understandable that he would compare his
Chinese princess to her. If we can credit Proverb with Merton's
poem "Hagia Sophia," we can perhaps credit his Chinese
princess with his fine books on Zen: *Zen and the Birds of Appetite*
(1968) and *Mystics and Zen Masters* (1967) as well as his poetic
renditions of Chuang Tzu, *The Way of Chuang Tzu* (1965).

The anima offers man the Eros (energy) to develop further his personality (a woman's animus performs a similar function for her), and it is often expressed in a burst of creativity. Merton's Chinese princess presents "freshness," "youth," "wonder," and "truth." In later life, men often fall in love with a younger woman and find themselves renewed, producing work of importance, if not genius. Artists like Yeats and Picasso are classic examples of such renewal, and Nabokov's *Lolita* is a fictional account of it. Merton, however, with his vow of celibacy, must rely on the inner woman.

The dream invigorates Merton. He knows "in my depths," that is, in his unconscious, that there is a figure who loves him for what he is, not just for his "everyday self," his ego and persona. He is loved for his *complete* self, which also includes the shadow. There is a suggestion, however, that his anima and his ego are not completely in tune with each other, that there are some aspects of Merton's anima that are still "unobtainable," perhaps referring to Merton's belief that he was incapable of loving or accepting love. Merton's journal entry about this dream reveals that he has analyzed it carefully, trying to understand what is "unobtainable." Jungian Marie Von France writes:

> But what does the role of the anima as guide to the inner world mean in practical terms? This positive function occurs when a man takes seriously the feelings, moods, expectations, and fantasies sent by the anima and when he fixes them in some form—for example, in writing, painting, sculpture, musical compositions, or dancing. When he works at this patiently and slowly, other more deeply unconscious material wells up from the depths and connects with the earlier material.[23]

❧

Merton records on August 8, 1961, the following dream:

Dream of being lost in a great city and walking "toward the center" without quite knowing where I was and suddenly coming to the road's end on a height overlooking a great bay, an arm of the harbor, and seeing a whole section of the city spread out before me on the hills, covered with light snow, realizing that, though I had far to go, I knew where I was because in this city there are two arms of the sea, which one always encounters and by which one can get one's direction.[24]

Merton's dream is an excellent example of what the individuation process, the journey toward wholeness, involves. As with the lost Dante's finding himself in a dark wood, Merton finds himself lost in a city (modern, urban imagery to be expected from a twentieth-century man). For a modern man, a modern metropolis would best represent the soul/psyche. He is walking "toward the center." This is a positive direction, for in Jungian psychology, the center is the Self: "The Self as a unifying principle within the human psyche occupies the central position of authority in relation to psychological life and, therefore, the destiny of the individual."[25]

When Merton's dream ego finds himself at a height, he sees before him an arm of the harbor. Water symbolizes the psyche. He has a view of the whole city; Merton is obliquely looking at himself, for the city is a collective of all that resides within Merton, including the anima and shadow archetypes. The snow indicates that certain aspects of his personality are still covered or hidden, but he at least knows "where I was." First, he was lost, and now he knows where he is; thus, progress has been made. The second part of the dream is as follows:

> Then, in a library of this city, speaking with strangers, I suddenly realize there is a charterhouse [Carthusian Monastery] here and that I have promised myself to visit and speak to the Prior about "my vocation." I ask someone, "Where is the charterhouse?" and he says, "I am just going to drive that way, I go right by it and I will take you." I accept this offer realizing that it is providential.[26]

The library is a place of books, therefore a place of knowledge. It is not surprising to find Merton, a writer and voracious reader, in a library. He is there to seek knowledge, particularly knowledge about himself. He is to visit the prior [the head of the Carthusian monastery] to discuss his vocation because in certain matters he may know where he is, but in others, he does not know. He needs *direction*. In fact, he does not know where the charterhouse is: "Where is the charterhouse?" His desire to enter a charterhouse has remained dormant (repressed) for many years, but it has again resurfaced both in his dreams and conscious mind. It seems that the dream is about to answer his problem, providing a shadow figure to drive "that way," but we have to be careful about shadow figures: They can be tricksters and can make us think that what we want is God's will, "providential." In the end, Merton was glad he hadn't transferred from Gethsemani to the Carthusians.[27]

❧

On September 12, 1961, Merton records the following dream:

> I am invited to a party. I meet some of the women going to the party, but there is estrangement. I am alone by the waterfront of a small town. A man says for

five dollars I can get across on a yacht to where I want to go. I have five dollars and more than five dollars, hundreds of dollars and also francs. I am conscious of my clerical garb. The yacht is a small schooner, a workaday schooner and no yacht. It does not move from the shore—we make it move a little pushing it from the inside, then I am out swimming ahead in the beautiful water, magic water, from the depths of which comes a wonderful life to which I am not entitled, a life and strength that I fear. I know that by diving in this water I can find something marvelous but that it is not fitting or right for me to dive as I am going to the further shore, with the strength that has come from the water, immortality.

Then in the summer house on the other side, where I have arrived first of all, I play with the dog and the child brings me two pieces of buttered white bread, which I am to eat on arrival.[28]

The salient feature is that the dream ego is estranged from "the women." This is a negative beginning: He is alone by the waterfront of a small town. To get across the water (the unconscious), he is offered an easy fee, and he accepts, though his efforts are needed to push the schooner out onto the surface of the water. This is not to be a deep encounter with his unconscious, only a skimming of the waters. He knows that in the depths of the water lies a "wonderful life," but he feels "not entitled" to it. Individuation requires work. He has not solved his "estrangement" from women; thus, he feels unworthy to receive the "strength" the water (unconscious) can provide, but it does, at least, help him make it to the other shore.

Playing with a dog and child indicates that he feels comfortable with his animal instincts and with his inner child; however, he is not yet a mature, integrated man. His efforts, however, to become one are rewarded with two pieces of buttered bread, a reminder of the Eucharist, spiritual nourishment. The buttered food will offer him strength, but it is not physical strength that he needs but *psychic* strength that is found within the unconscious.

What may have inhibited his diving into the waters to encounter his unconscious is his awareness of his "clerical garb." The priest/monk is too aware of his inhibiting persona. If he could strip himself of personae, he could dive into the waters, the "magic water." Why magic? Water can cleanse, it can cause rebirth and connect with life, with others. The dream figure remains Adam—without an Eve.

Could the reference to a child on the opposite shore be an oblique reference to the child Merton abandoned in England when he came to America?

❧

On February 4, 1965, Merton records the following dream:

Last night I had a curious and moving dream about a "black mother." I was in a place somewhere I had been as a child. I could not recognize it, but also there seemed to be some connection with Bell Hollow and I realized that I had come there for a reunion with a Negro foster mother whom I had loved in my child-hood in the dream. Indeed it seemed in the dream, that I owed my life to her, to her love for me, so that it was really she and not my natural mother who had given me life, as if from her had come a new life. And there she was. Her face was ugly and severe, yet great warmth came from her to me and what I recognized was not her face but the warmth of her embrace and

her heart, so to speak. Then we danced a little together,
I and my black mother.[29]

Merton was very much concerned with racism in America
in the 1960s, and he wrote eloquently about the civil rights
movement. His poems "And the Children of Birmingham" and
"Picture of a Black Child with a White Doll" reveal his great compassion and empathy for the suffering of black children at the
hands of white racists. One of his best friends (Merton's official
biographer who died before completing his work) was John
Howard Griffin, the author of the best-seller *Black Like Me*
(1961). A black anima figure certainly points to an identification
with African Americans (a term, of course, not used in Merton's
time) in his conscious life; it also illustrates Merton's continuing
all-embracing attitude toward the world, which began with his
Louisville Vision.

In his published autobiography, Merton says very little
about his mother. In the original manuscript, he had written
more about his mother, but when told to edit the book, which
was too long, he cut out sections about his mother and kept
those about his father.

In this dream the black mother is described as having a face
that is "severe." This is the exact word Merton uses to describe
his natural mother, but there is a difference in the black mother:
She exudes warmth, unlike his natural mother, who was portrayed as a distant mother, intellectually interested in observing
her son's development, but perhaps miserly in her expression of
affection and love.

A black and "ugly" anima figure is one that need not attract
by being white or beautiful. In Western culture, darkness is often
interpreted as evil, and white beauty is held as the ideal of feminine
perfection. But whiteness and beauty are not the essence of the
feminine. In this dream, Merton is not duped by appearances and

accepts the gifts of the feminine, which are love and warmth. He feels her love in their embrace, symbolic of the archetype *coniunctio*, suggesting the union of opposites, transformation and rebirth.

The dream ego's dance with his black mother enhances their union and harmony: Subject and object have become one. Maybe Merton has finally come to terms with his severe mother or, on a deeper level, accepts the reality that although his mother appeared to be demanding and severe, she really did love him, that she herself, like her son, was uncomfortable in expressing love, but the love was always here. Thus, Merton feels a "deep gratitude." The dance is also symbolic, its motion is circular, and for Jung, the circle is a symbol of completeness.

The reference to Bell Hollow concerns a piece of land that Gethsemani was considering purchasing for hermitages. Merton lyrically describes the area as a pristine place where the water is pure and the air clean; in fact, it is Edenic. It is the land of his black mother. Such a positive dream can only mean that Merton is entering new territories of self-discovery and self-realization, a land of milk and honey (Exod 3:8).

Perhaps here is the place to mention a poem, "The Sting of Conscience," in which Merton projects his shadow onto his natural mother. He writes it after reading Graham Greene's novel *The Quiet American*.

> You have written, Greene, in your last book
> The reasons why I so hate milk.
> You have diagnosed the war in my own gut
> Against the innocence, yes, against the dead mother
> My famous refuge.[30]

Merton and his agent Naomi Burton got into an argument about whether or not this poem should be published. According to Patrick O'Connell, on June 4, Merton obviously defensive, admits he is projecting his troubles onto his mother, America, the monastery, and the church. She felt it should not be published, and he finally admitted it was too neurotic. It has not been included in his *Collected Poems*. Is it perhaps too revelatory?

❧

On November 19, 1968, at the Mim Tea Estate, Merton records the following dream:

> Last night I had a curious dream about Kanchenjunga. I was looking at the mountain and it was pure white, absolutely pure, especially the peaks that lie to the west. And I saw the pure beauty of their shape and outline, all in white. And I heard a voice saying—or got the clear idea of: "There is another side to the mountain." I realized that it was turned around and everything was lined up differently; I was seeing it from the Tibetan side. This morning my quarrel with the mountain is ended. Not that it is a big love affair—but why get mad at a mountain. It is beautiful, chastely white in the morning sun—and right in view of the bungalow window.
>
> There is another side of Kanchenjunga and of every mountain—the side that has never been photographed and turned into postcards. That is the side worth seeing.[31]

Holy mountains appear throughout the history of man in general and in the Bible in particular. We think of Mount Olympus and Mount Sinai. Mountains are considered sacred places: the higher they are, the closer to God. Thus, men want to climb them, for they are symbolic of man's search for the spiritual, for God.

Merton's dream ego is gazing at Mount Kanchenjunga. It is dazzling in white snow, the snow at the peak even whiter (we think of Merton in his habit: snow-white alb and cowl with black scapular). The mountain's beauty impresses the dream ego, so pure is its shape and outline. The mountain represents the spiritual ascent, one the dreamer is actively involved with in his conscious life, having come from the West to the East, a journey part and parcel of his own spiritual journey. His inner voice tells him that there is another side of the mountain, suddenly now turned around to reveal its Tibetan side, likely a reference to his recent meeting with the Dalai Lama in 1968, one of the world's great spiritual masters. It could also signify Merton's new interest in the Tibetan religion (Buddhism), one of the results of his meeting with the Dalai Lama.

The two sides of the mountain represent the conscious and unconscious mind. Or the dream may be referring to the persona, the side of ourselves we present to the world, the photographed side for which we pose, the kind of photography made into postcards, representing the false self, not the True Self. The side Merton is interested in is the side not photographed: the unknown Self residing within the center of the unconscious, which he calls the True Self. The ego and persona are represented by the photograph, the Self by the side not photographed: the seen and the unseen.

He refers to a quarrel. What specifically is the quarrel? Is it that he did not want to admit there are two sides of the mountain? Is there an unwillingness to accept that there are two selves: one we present to the world, the other kept hidden (shadow), the part of ourselves we ignore but should explore if we are to become whole human beings?

In this dream, Merton suggests that he is more interested in the Tibetan religion, specifically Mahayana Tibetan Buddhism, than he may be aware of consciously. It also reveals that he knows there are still parts of himself that he has yet to learn about: "the other side of the mountain." To admit this idea in a dream underlines the utter importance of Merton's search for the True Self, a search that continued until his sudden death in Bangkok. He likely recorded the dream to remind himself about the importance of his spiritual journey.

Merton, after his meeting with the Dalai Lama, viewed mountains differently: He saw them as mandala (that is, a symbolic circular figure, generally representing self-unity) symbols: "One instinctively sees the mountain as a mandala, slightly askew no doubt, with a central presence and surrounding presences more or less amiable."[32] Thinking in terms of a mandala is new for Merton. Jung says,

> The contemplation of a mandala is meant to bring inner peace, a feeling that life has again found its meaning and order. The mandala also conveys this feeling when it appears spontaneously in the dreams of modern men who are not influenced by any religious tradition of this sort and know nothing about it. Perhaps the positive effect is even greater in such cases because knowledge and tradition sometimes blur or even block the spontaneous experience.[33]

This positive dream is the last one recorded in his journals, a beautiful one to say the least.

# Chapter Seven

*The Strange Islands* (1957) contains poems that were mostly written in 1955–56 during Dom Sortais's ban on Merton's journal writing and during another stability crisis. It is a transitional work, exhibiting a transformation in Merton's poetry. Missing are the didacticism, the *contemptus mundi*, and the florid imagery of his earlier poetry. In their place, he offers devotion, monastic silence, joy, and simplicity; furthermore, he has adopted an ascetic poetic line reminiscent of William Carlos Williams (but not as stark as his friend Robert Lax's verse).

"New Directness" is what renders *The Strange Islands* a radiant book even though some poems address Merton's continual though not continuous struggle with depression. Merton employs a new, lucid, pure line, one that pierces to the core of his being; thus, we have a portrait of a man still struggling to understand the stranger (shadow) within, often projected onto the world, the shadow that obscures his True Self, who is Christ.

Merton always considered himself a poet first and foremost, for poetry became his locus of self-definition, not only as a poet but also as a man of spirit. The long poem "Elias—Variations on a Theme" represents the landscape of his soul. Its verses are like "pathways": transcending "geography" of stanza and verse, they chart the inner journey.

Such a journey demands elimination of the extraneous. The stripped, unadorned language of "Elias" corresponds to the stripping away of ego to allow the revelation of the True Self. The desert setting of Merton's journey implies the discarding of the superficial;

the spiritual journey purges one of the false, symbolized by a land-scape where "the pine burns" and the sun is "furious." Merton writes that "the climate in which monastic prayer flowers is that of the desert, where the comfort of man is absent, where the secure routines of man's city offer no support, and where prayer must be sustained by God in the purity of faith."[1] Merton wrote "Elias" when he was allowed to use a red trailer hermitage the abbey aban-doned in the woods. One must travel down a dirt path, which leads to a deeper wood, which seemingly "dies." It is an area where one could easily become lost.

One must question Merton's preference to abide in such a bleak landscape. In the mid-1950s when Merton composed "Elias," he had been searching for more solitude and silence in his monastic life (enduring another crisis). His fame as a spiritual writer had ironically nearly destroyed his original purpose in entering Gethsemani "to disappear into God." Although the landscape *appears* to be bleak —having a "winter sun" (the poem was written in December 1954), a "pathway" that "dies," and wildness, "wilds begin"—it is the site where Merton can "find" his soul. The bird is symbolic of the soul; it can, indeed, take flight in this stripped, wild land where the "ground is warm" and the bird sings "alone."

In Merton's vast poetic corpus, "Elias" is the desert poem par excellence (Mott says "In Silence" was Merton's first desert poem, but "Elias" was written two years before "In Silence"),[2] and critic George Woodcock describes "Elias" as the best of the desert poems, or as William Carlos Williams might term it, "The Desert Music."[3]

Just as the ancients sequestered themselves in the desert for a silent, solitary encounter with God, so too Merton has entered the Kentucky woods—the closest alternative to a desert experi-ence available to an American monk. Such an exterior landscape is a prompt for a Trappist monk—he prays to be purged of all that is not of God. His only visible companions are natural: the blunt pine, the winter sun, the dying pathway, and the solitary bird, imagery suggesting the purgative stage of the mystical journey.

Merton has been contemplating the desert long before he composed "Elias." He writes:

> Elias was a man like unto us....His strength may be glorified in the transformation of our weakness....We feel his eyes upon us as we sit under the fig tree, and our souls momentarily springs to life at the touch of his hidden finger. This flash of fire is our solitude, yet it binds us to our brethren....It remains for us to recognize the mystery that your heart is my hermitage and that the only way I can enter into the desert is by learning our burden and having of my own....
>
> What is my new desert? The name of it is *compassion*. There is no wilderness so terrible, so beautiful, so arid and so fruitful as the wilderness of compassion....Do you suppose I have a spiritual life? I have none, I am indigence, I am silence, I am poverty, I am solitude, for I have renounced spirituality to find God...I die of love for you, Compassion: I take you for my Lady, as Francis married poverty, I marry you, the Queen of hermits, and the Mother of the poor.[4]

At first, the natural setting appears to be hostile and unappealing, but Merton affirms that the "ground is warm." The ground is warm from the sun, but it is also warm and friendly because the earth is hospitable, hence, Mother Earth. Merton's love of nature is a reminder that he has read and admired the poet Thoreau, who also chose to live a hermit's life at the edge of Walden Pond. In his own way, Merton lives a Thoreauvian life.

The difference between the austere New Englander and the Trappist is that Merton does not seek a vague transcendental communion with nature, but the mystical union with God, as is described in *The Imitation of Christ*.

Merton imagines himself as Elias, an Old Testament prophet of the northern kingdom during the reign of King Ahab. He had been sent by God to chastise Ahab for encouraging the worship of Baal, a pagan god of storm and rain (1Kgs 16:31–33). In the midst of the three-year famine, God commands the despairing Elias to depart and to live by himself. Elias stations himself under a juniper tree near water where ravens, by God's command, provide him with daily bread.

Later, Elias finds his way to Mount Horeb where he spends the night in a cave. He attentively listens for God's voice until God reveals himself, not in powerful thunder or lightning, but in a gentle, barely audible breeze. Elias's life, therefore, is symbolic of the contemplative life of waiting and listening.

Merton's command to himself via Elias is to *listen*, the first word in the Rule of St. Benedict. Merton becomes a monk to listen to the word of God in silence and solitude. His daily life, however, is entangled in a myriad of issues he could not have foreseen: He is an international best-selling author; the demand for more books grows, and Merton surrenders himself to producing them at a fast pace. He is also pursued by scores of people: ordinary people seeking spiritual counsel, people with personal problems, intellectuals seeking dialogue, and the famous reaching out to touch base with another renowned figure.

His inner self, however, quietly reminds the young "prophet" to listen. But listen to *what*? To the "southern wind"? To the "wind and rain"? To the "woods" and the "ground"? He listens to God's creation; it is a model of conforming to the will of God. The wind blows, the rain falls, the bird sings, the sun grows pale, and the desert ground also follows its calling, as he writes, to be warm.

Elias, an alias for Merton, *must* follow his vocation—he must exquisitely listen, for God rarely leaves "miraculous" signs of his presence. He "bends no blade, no fern." Elias looks, but sees nothing; a breeze, however, is invisible and can only be heard. Prayer, therefore, is exquisite hearing—listening to the still, small voice.

Merton describes the sun as "furious"; it is symbolic of purgation. The desert fathers went into the desert to fast and to pray in imitation of John the Baptist and Jesus Christ. Theirs was a harshly ascetic life lived where the sun burned away all that interferes with their relationship with God. It cleanses the soul, rendering it more worthy of God's presence. Perhaps there is here a suggestion that Merton, too, is "furious," angered by his own false worship of fame, his failure to follow his contemplative vocation.

Elias gathers Ahab and the false prophets of Baal at Mount Carmel to prove the identity of the true God. He commands that two altars be built for the sacrifice of two bulls. The Baalan prophets call upon their god to send down fire to consume their offering, but nothing happens. Elias builds his altar of wood and stone and places on it a bull, drenching everything in water. The fire of the Lord falls, consuming the offering along with the wood and the stones and the dust, and it licks up the water (1 Kgs 18:1–40).

Merton has no need to prove the identity of God, no need to prove which prophets are the true prophets. He is not called upon to set fire to an offering, but he is called to *be* an offering—to sacrifice his self for God. Such an offering is the core of his monastic vocation—sacrificing the ego for the love of God. The ego is to be burned away by the "furious sun." The sun is relentless because Merton's false self remains intact despite the desert landscape.

Merton does not know where the "fields end." He does not know where the "stars begin." This echoes Merton's famous prayer, "My Lord God I have no idea where I am going, I do not see the road ahead of me, I cannot know where it will end." Such geographical and astronomical knowledge is unnecessary in the pursuit of God. To know where the field ends and the stars begin is to know the whole journey. Such knowledge is not available in time—only in eternity.

To pursue God, Merton need only "listen." The "seed sleeps" brings to mind the symbolic potential we all possess to listen to the voice of God. The "winter rain" will nourish the seed, but the seed's fruition depends on how much of life-giving water it absorbs; thus, Merton suggests a listening to everything: the wind, the rain, the woods, the ground—the "ground of being" because God is omnipresent.

Merton's poem is perhaps a response to several of T. S. Eliot's poems, specifically "The Hollow Men," also a desert poem in which Eliot describes the hollow men's setting as a "cactus land," lying under the "twinkle of a fading star." The difference between Merton and Eliot's poems is that Merton is a man of faith and hope whereas Eliot (before his Christian conversion in 1927) is a man of despair, his faith nothing but "the twinkle of a fading star." For Eliot the desert is also a place of purification, of diminishment, of stripping, of kenosis (emptying), of silence, of solitude. The desert becomes the locus, not of a deadened landscape, but of a soulscape where there can be rebirth, leading to an encounter with the Divine.

## The Chariot as a Red Trailer

Although written long after the composition of "Elias," the following journal entry sheds light on Merton's love of the prophet Elias: "The icon of St. Elias which Jack Ford brought me from St. Meinrad's, and which yesterday I put up on the east wall [of the hermitage]. Fabulously beautiful and delicate and strong. A great red transparent globe of light, with angelic horses rearing in unison, and angels lifting all of it up to the blackness of the divine mystery....What a thing to have by you! It changes everything! Transfigures everything!"[5]

"Variation II" addresses the biblical story of the prophet Elias's being taken up to heaven in a chariot of fire. Merton's own chariot of fire (his rusty trailer) is not one surrounded by "spirits of flame." There are no "supernatural wings"—just the wings of local birds and no "grand machines." It is an ordinary red trailer.

For Merton much depends, to paraphrase William Carlos Williams, on his red trailer; although it is not a miraculous fiery chariot, it is the "hermitage" for Merton to pursue silence, to pursue solitude, to write poetry, a place to sit, to wait, and to listen for the voice of God.

Merton desires nothing extraordinary—in fact, he prefers the "old wagon / With the wet, smashed wheels." He needs nothing to boost his ego. He is not Elias, he is not a prophet with a "chariot of fire"; he is a monk with an "old trailer / With the dead stove in it." So there will be no flaming, flying chariot, only a "derelict" trailer that moves nowhere, remaining "[b]ehind the felled oaks, faster, burning nothing." The setting of "felled oaks" is the one preferred by the fallen man, Merton, the monk and poet. By rejecting ostentation (a fiery chariot) to embrace humility (a derelict trailer) and choosing "wet, smashed wheels" over "supernatural wings," Merton affirms who he is: a contemplative Trappist monk. The red trailer, therefore, symbolizes the kind of person Merton is before God: a humble, imperfect man.

The red trailer is soaked in rainwater as "the rain comes down the pipe and covers the floor." The rain symbolizes purification, baptism, and transformation; in short, the "old trailer" becomes Merton's place of rebirth; it is "The House of God / The Gate of Heaven." The trailer suffices; consequently, there is no reason for him to travel anywhere beyond his own hermitage.

In a larger sense the trailer can be likened to the Abbey of Gethsemani itself where Merton renounces all to become a humble monk. Within the enclosure of the abbey, Merton devotes his life to burning away all that is false—by the fire of purification, of asceticism, and of prayer (cf. the last lines of *The Seven Storey Mountain*).

## The "Naked" Merton

Early in his monastic and poetic career the symbol of seeds becomes rooted in Merton's mind. In the opening of his first book of spiritual direction, he declares that in every moment of our lives seeds are implanted in our souls. Many of these *divine* seeds perish because they fall upon poor earth, people unprepared to receive and cultivate them. Merton says:

> Every moment and every event of man's life on earth plants something in his soul. For just as the wind carries thousands of invisible and visible winged seeds, so the stream of time brings with it germs of spiritual vitality that come to rest imperceptibly in the minds and wills of men.[6]

The seed represents the inner life with an inner center where the True Self is encountered. The seed symbolizes the potential every Christian possesses to touch and be touched by the Divine. The seeds "hide"; they grow in secret, these "seeds of contemplation," but they possess the potential to grow and to flower into fruit. Seeds are unlike the lifeless stones, "inanimate things," that cover the earth. They are also solitary, containing within them no seed that will someday grow, remaining "alone forever."

The seed "waits to grow and bear / Fruit." This is a New Testament reference to "a tree is known by its fruit" (Luke 6:43). The seed must be patient; it waits, grows, and finally bears fruit. The spiritual life, too, has its own holy rhythm and maturation.

Merton stresses the spiritual "way" of waiting. Waiting also implies *listening*. Only by waiting *and* listening to the "still, small voice" will we grow and mature as Christians. But we must do our waiting and listening in a certain spirit: We must *care*. To care suggests involvement, nurturing attention—all of which is done preferably in silent secrecy. The seed hides in the ground, to burst forth through the earth later, and make known its presence, and offer its fruit (cf. Dylan Thomas's "The Force That Through the Green Fuse Drives").

We find in Merton's essay "Philosophy of Solitude" (written at approximately the same time as "Elias") a description of the kind of man he hopes to become:

> The emptiness of the true solitary is marked then by a great simplicity. This simplicity can be deceptive, because it may be hidden under a surface of apparent complexity, but it is there nevertheless, behind the outer contradictions of the man's life. It manifests itself in a kind of candor though he may be very reticent. Here is in this lonely one a gentleness, a deep sympathy, though he may be apparently antisocial. There is a great purity of love, though he may hesitate to manifest his love in any way, or to commit himself openly to it.[7]

In this section, Merton stresses the themes of emptiness, despair, and exhaustion. Rain, symbolic of God's mercy, arrives "to fix" the "exhausted mountain." (Here, we cannot help thinking of Merton as the "exhausted mountain" of *The Seven Storey*

*Mountain.* Having grown so much spiritually, did Merton see himself as having once been a false prophet in his autobiography?) The rain refreshes and renews because it knows what is false and what is true. Here, the full weight of his calling as monk and poet seems to press upon Merton. Again, he chides himself for not having the "patience of a rock or tree," for not *listening*. If he had listened more attentively, perhaps he might not have been trapped in the "persona of prophet." False prophets have their own cities where "[t]hey want to receive you / Because you are not sent to them."

But, as with all good things, rain comes from God. Rain falls as does grace in our spiritual lives. It "descends" to refresh and renew us when we are truly exhausted or most spiritually arid.

Then follows a description of a post-World War II society trapped in a new form of combat, the cold war—a place with "its own division," of "diversion and war," of "misery"; a place where people "cannot stand to be too well." This is the place for false prophets and for persons who choose their own anguish, a place where people blame their unhappiness on others.

Merton divests himself of Elias's prophetic persona. We see the "naked" Merton, the monk and poet looking at himself directly—and not liking what he sees. It takes courage and blunt, if not brutal, honesty to face the false self in the interior mirror of the True Self. Again, Merton perceives that he has been a "man without silence."

Although sequestered in a monastery, Merton confesses to being a part of this modern world, and he chastises himself for being unfaithful to his ideal of a hidden life, "And I have been a man without silence, / A man without patience, with too many / Questions." Merton also accuses himself of not being "patient." He always feels the need to seek *more* solitude and silence, not at his own abbey but elsewhere—the West Coast, Mexico,

Alaska, Latin America, and often as a Carthusian. His abbot, however, urges Merton to be patient and to wait upon the Lord.

Merton's "blaming" is certainly a reference to his earlier judgmental tendency. Of course, he now recognizes that throwing stones at others is not Christlike, and it accomplishes nothing. In both his autobiography and in the first edition of *Seeds of Contemplation*, Merton projects much of his own shadow onto society, seeing "the world" as dangerous and evil. He gradually learns that all people, whether within or without the abbey, are not very different, and that *everyone* requires God's love and mercy.

Throughout "Elias," Merton tries to keep his feet on the ground (particularly Gethsemani's ground). No ascending chariots for him. Keeping his ego grounded, however, demands a constant examination of conscience that often finds its way into his poetry and journals. He accuses himself of arrogance: "Someone accused me of being a 'high priest of creativity.' Or at least of allowing people to regard me as one. This is perhaps true....*The sin of wanting to be a pontiff* [Merton's emphasis], of wanting to be heard, of wanting converts, disciples. Being in a cloister I thought I did not want this. Of course I did, and everyone knows it....I have got to face the fact that there is in me a desire for survival as pontiff, prophet, and writer, and this has to be renounced before I can be myself at last."[8]

Thus, composing poetry is a sacramental act for Merton. His verse becomes the confessional where he records his failures in the hope that such confessions will lead him toward self-knowledge and a deeper understanding of his inner journey.

He also refers to "my own city." What city? Cosmopolitan London? Louisville, Kentucky? Cambridge? New York? He asks, "Am I better off than inhabitants of these cities?" Merton's conclusion is negative. He is not a saint, not even a modern prophet. He remains the "broken" Merton seeking God's perfection while "facing the sound of distant guns" (a reference to nearby Fort Knox). He is a man in search of his True Self.

Perhaps the most important message of his early book *Seeds of Contemplation* is Merton's emphasis of the false and True Self. He wrote, "Every one of us is shadowed by an illusory person: a false self." This image of the self, Merton asserts, is one that "exists only in my own egocentric desires."[9] Our True Self is anchored in Christ. The more Christlike we become, the more we are our True Selves.

# A Free Man

In the fourth variation, Merton is alone under a pine tree, alone because the inner journey is a solitary one. Merton has stripped himself of one false self: "I who am not sent." He is not a God-sent prophet like Elias, just an ordinary man. The "pathway dies" for the real journey is within.

The "blunt pine" suggests the "tree of knowledge" in the Garden of Eden; it also calls to mind the tree of the cross of Christ, "the Wisdom of God and the Power of God" (1 Cor 1:24). The appearance of trees as an image, according to Carl Jung, is often symbolic of the general archetype of transformation, suggesting rootedness, repose, growth, and fruition, as well as a union of earth and sky.

Merton's diminutive, sometimes evanescent, imagery—seed, salt, snow, cell, and drops of rain—all suggest that embarking on the inner journey requires one to be humble, small. It is necessary to know one's own nothingness. Merton's verse echoes T. S. Eliot's verse from the *Four Quartets* that states the only wisdom we can hope to acquire is the wisdom of humility. "Humility is endless," Eliot writes.

"The free man is not alone as busy men are." A "free man" is not as "busy men," getting and spending. He sings "[a]lone as universes do." He is poetically one with the universe; he is an integrated man. The freedom and harmony of wholeness is "clear, unmistakable" when it is achieved. This wholeness also reaches out to others, to the universe.

> To belong to God I have to belong to myself. I have to be alone—at least interiorly alone. This means the constant renewal of a decision. I cannot belong to people. None of me belongs to anybody but God. Absolute loneliness of the imagination, the memory, the will. My love for everybody is equal, neutral and clean. No exclusiveness. Simple and *free* as the sky because I love everybody and am possessed by nobody, not held, not bound....They can have Thomas Merton. He's dead. Fr. Louis, he's half dead too. For my part my name is that sky, those fence posts and those cedar trees (my emphasis).[10]

Why a "blunt pine"? "Blunt" suggests honesty. A person must be honest with himself in order to achieve spiritual wholeness; it comes from following "[h]is own pattern." To become whole (holy), he must win "his wide field," as well as an increased awareness of his true center, which is Christ: "with God in the Center." Thus, the "wide field" corresponds with an enlightened person, whose soul expands and centers in God: a person of psychic and spiritual wholeness.

The final verse of "Elias" is separated from the rest of the poem for emphasis:

> For a free man's road has neither beginning nor end.

Who finally is the "free man"? Merton's description of such a man is as follows:

...Now my whole life is this—to keep unencumbered. The wind owns the fields where I walk, and I own nothing and am owned by nothing, and I shall never even be forgotten because no one will ever discover me....I seek no face. I treasure no experience, no memory. Anything I write down here is only for guidance because of my constant gravitation away from solitude. It will remind me how to go home. Not to be like the man who looked in the glass and straightway forgot what manner of man he was. But at the same time not to be remembering myself lest I come to remember the person I am not.[11]

In this last verse there is again an echo of T. S. Eliot's *Four Quartets*: "In my beginning is my end....In my end is my beginning." The free person's road *is* God: God who is the Alpha and the Omega, God without beginning or end. The verse also serves as an answer to Eliot's constructive criticism of Merton's verse, for "Elias" is not hastily composed, one of Eliot's criticisms, and Merton's language is now exquisitely precise. He has the *right* to call himself a poet.

🍐

Why was "Elias" so important to Merton? For an answer, we need only turn to a journal entry for November 29, 1951,

Elias was a man like unto us....Day after day the outward man crumbles and breaks down and the inward man, the Man of Heaven, is born and grows in wisdom and knowledge before the eyes of men—who cannot recognize him....And yet we suspect His presence in the mystery which is not revealed to the wise and prudent. We feel His eyes upon us as we sit under the fig tree and our souls momentarily spring to life at the touch of His hidden finger. This flash of fire is our solitude, but it binds us to our brethren. It is the fire that has quickened the Mystical Body since Pentecost so that every Christian is, at the same time, a hermit and the whole church, and we are all members one of another. It remains for us to recognize the mystery that your heart is my hermitage and that the only way I can enter into the desert is by bearing your burden and leaving you my own.[12]

Although Merton's "Elias" is a breakthrough poem, not only in poetic style but also in insightful soul-searching, Merton is still not immune to being dragged into bouts of self-loathing and depression, as is shown by the following poem:

### Whether There Is Enjoyment in Bitterness

This afternoon, let me
Be a sad person. Am I not
Permitted (like other men)
To be sick of myself?

Am I not allowed to be hollow,
Or fall in the hole
Or break my bones (within me)
In the trap set by my own
Lie to myself? O my friend,
I too must sin and sin.

I too must hurt other people and
(Since I am no exception)
I must be hated by them.

Do not forbid me, therefore
To taste the same bitter poison.
And drink the gall that love
(Love most of all) so easily becomes.

Do not forbid me (once again) to be
Angry, bitter, disillusioned
Wishing I could die.

While life and death
Are killing one another in my flesh,
Leave me in peace. I can enjoy,
Even as other men, this agony.

Only (whoever you may be)
Pray for my soul. Speak my name
To Him, for in my bitterness
I hardly speak to Him: and He
While He is busy killing me
Refuses to listen.[13]

This poem, written during Merton's stay at Collegeville, Minnesota, where he goes on July 22, 1956, to participate in a conference on psychiatry and Religious life, and where he has his famous (or infamous depending on how one interprets it) encounter with Dr. Gregory Zilboorg, in my opinion, is the portrait of a depressed man—or at the very least, a depressed neurotic. Few poems in Merton's corpus (excluding his love poems, *Eighteen Poems*) are so nakedly confessional. Merton, like all of us, has his "bad days." Depression as a mood is part of the human condition, one Merton fully understands, having dealt with it when he was young, losing both his mother and his father to cancer. There was also that day in a hotel room when the window beckoned to him to consider killing himself. Merton, to borrow Robert Frost's phrase, is well acquainted with the Night. Monica Furlong observes that, compared to his prose work, his poetry is obscure, as if written in an incomprehensible code, perhaps to keep his superiors (abbot and censors) ignorant of his actual state of mind.[14]

Notice the poem's diction: *poison*, *gall*, *angry*, *disillusioned*, *bitterness*, and *agony*, all suggesting a person in spiritual and psychological pain. How long has he been depressed? Of course, we can only guess.

We recall Merton's difficult past: in 1936 on the Long Island Railroad and later his breakdown around the time of his ordination, the stability crisis of 1952, and now this emotional crisis.

Merton's poem (and excerpts) may have been the result of one of these boiling times, these periods of depression. The poem and the excerpts reveal a man's struggling for wholeness. He understands that his doubts, fears, anger, sadness, depressions, guilt, and resentment are all part of his life, and he accepts them and thanks God for them.

Yet how poignant it is to hear Merton plead, "let me / Be a sad person." We should keep in mind that his poem is written after a debilitating encounter with Zilboorg, the well-known psychiatrist; we sympathize with Merton's humanity, with his vulnerability. He is "sick of myself" or rather sick of the mask he constructs for himself: the perfect Catholic writer/monk, the holy eremite, the Catholic apologist, the spotless priest. These are all the masks with which he lived. Even the notion that he is a "saint" hovers in the air, and many of his readers are in awe of the prolific Catholic writer and his beautiful books about spirituality.

In *this* poem, however, Merton reminds his readers that he too is made of bones, he too is a sinner, he too is a person who inadvertently hurts people. He is in effect saying, "I am just like

you: a flawed, imperfect human being. And because I am so broken as a human being, I too get sad." *Sad* may well be a code
word for depressed. The sadness (depression) can be so severe,
he would rather die than live. He candidly admits to a maudlin
self-pity, but he is also humble enough to ask for the prayers of
others: "Pray for my soul / Speak my name / To Him, for in my
bitterness / I hardly speak to Him."

He confesses, "I too must hurt other people." Whom has he
hurt? Is it the girl with whom he fathered a child, abandoning
both of them in England while he escaped to America? Or is he
referring to a more recent wounding of a person? Merton tried to
help one of the novices through the use of psychology, a field in
which he was not trained. He writes:

> I learned lately (around the time "Enjoyment in Bitter-
> ness" was written) that one of the novices whom we
> thought neurotic and who was indeed disturbed, was
> disturbed largely by the bars and illusions that had
> arisen in his relations with me—he became very
> upset fancying that I demanded that he be a brilliant
> and complicated person (which is what he fancies me
> to be) and I enhanced that illusion by not giving time
> to talk about himself but always delivering the diag-
> nosis before he had even a chance to tell me all the
> symptoms. This, while beating him down and ren-
> dering him very insecure, also stimulated a desperate
> search for more "symptoms" so that I could deliver
> more and more godlike diagnoses....Finally, in a cul-
> mination of stupidity I even gave him the Rorshach
> Test (I had been encouraged by Dr. Kisker) and inter-
> preted it all wrong.[15]

The word *bitterness* in the poem's title grabs our attention. Why is Merton (or his narrator) bitter? Michael Mott writes:

> By July 30, the abbot had arrived for the last few days of the conference. When Merton wrote later that the stability crisis of 1955 had been resolved by his own ineptitude and the "adroit politics of my superiors," he was most bitter about the part the abbot had played. By July 1956, Merton knew of the letter Dom James had written to Archbishop Montini on May 16, 1955, which implied that Father Louis was temperamentally unstable, too artistically volatile to be entrusted with determining his own spiritual destiny.[16]

Dom Fox's letter reveals that he is a man intent on keeping Merton at Gethsemani. He is not loath to suggesting that Merton's leaving Gethsemani might cause a scandal in the church. Monica Furlong is correct to suspect Fox worked against him behind the scenes. Dom Fox was not being honest with Merton about Zilboorg and about his secret maneuvers to prevent Merton's transfer to another religious community, and about what he actually wrote to the future pope, Paul VI, Archbishop Giovanni Battisa Montini.

Zilboorg orchestrates his meeting Merton at the conference at St. John's. Let us examine what Zilboorg said to Merton.

> This morning before mass I talked an hour and a half with Zilboorg about my own troubles and a lot of things came out.

> 1. It turns out *he* was the one who *engineered* my coming here—through Abbot Baldwin—partly because of the danger of the article being published ("Neurosis

in Monastic Life") and partly because he had sensed my difficulties.

2. It turns out also—as I know—that I am in somewhat bad shape and that I am neurotic—and that the difficulties handling it right is very considerable. He has his own ideas about that—God alone knows if they are feasible.

3. Great extent of my dependence on vows—I would hardly have imagined I used them in the way he said, but anyway, I can get some details on it. As substitutes for reality?

4. "You are a gadfly to your superiors....Very stubborn—you keep coming back until you get what you want....You are afraid to be an ordinary monk in the community....You and Father Eudes can easily become a pair of semi-psychotic quacks....Talking to Dr. Rome (about Zen) you thought only of yourself using him as a source of information and self-aggrandizement....You thought nothing at all of your priesthood, the apostolate, the church, his soul.... You like to be famous, you want to be a big shot, you keep pushing your way out—to publicity— Megalomania and narcissism are your big trends.... Your hermit trend is pathological....It is not intelligence you lack, but affectivity"—meaning it is there but I have never let it get out—so that when the situation calls for it I either intellectualize—verbalize— or else go into a *depression* (emphasis added).

And finally, "It will do you no good to be forbidden to write—you need some silence and isolation, but it needs to be prohibited in your heart—if it is merely forbidden, it will not seem prohibited to you—Yet

> your writing is now becoming verbological—but your
> words must be incarnate.[17]

There is obviously much said by Zilboorg to make Merton "bitter" (perhaps also a code word for "depressed"), much of it unfair, and apparently based on a cursory reading of Merton's books. This is the first time the two had ever met. There is, strangely enough, another long gap in Merton's journals from September 12, 1956, to April 4, 1957. We wonder if Merton had seriously followed Zilboorg's recommendation about not writing.

    Mott is, I think, correct to say, "Zilboorg seemed to have some preconceptions about Merton even before the meeting at St. John's. In New York, Zilboorg states that he has already analyzed Merton from his published writings. He feels confident he knew what the trouble was."[18] Could Zilboorg himself have been involved in shadow projection? Zilboorg is also a well-known figure, a former actor who much enjoyed the limelight. Merton may be justified about being "sad" (yet another possible code word for "depressed") about such a negative description of himself, especially if his own abbot—literally, "father"—is involved in the seemingly arranged confrontation (you can't "engineer" anything without the cooperation of *someone* at Gethsemani).

    The second meeting with Zilboorg, with the abbot present, is so painful for Merton that he weeps in front of both Abbot Fox and Zilboorg. Further evidence of the pain of this confrontation is that Merton does not record it in his journal. (Abbot Fox already had written to Archbishop Montini, recommending that Merton is too unstable to leave Gethsemani. Merton, this time, *is* aware of the letter.)

    From a Jungian perspective, the poem is illustrative of Merton's individuation, of coming to terms with his humanity as well as the integration of shadow aspects of his personality, but such efforts do not rule out the dis-ease of clinical depression.

Depression can rear its ugly head when we least expect it, and when it comes, sometimes the best way to handle it is somehow to embrace it—for when we *integrate* it, we will not fear it, and ultimately it is a way to greater self-knowledge, which in turn leads to greater psychological wholeness.

Merton offers his readers an excruciatingly honest portrait of himself: a portrait of naked vulnerability. He wears no mask: He simply and candidly says that this poem is about "me." "The Anatomy of Melancholy," a poem discussed later, also addresses depression. In it he hides himself by referring to a nameless person, "There was a man"; the man is obviously Merton himself. Why the camouflage? In the 1950s there was still a very real stigma (to *this* reader, at least) to admitting that one suffered from depression. It was socially all right to be "sad," and it was still acceptable to admit to "melancholy," but the very word *depression* had at all costs to be avoided. It must be noted, however, that in his unexpurgated journals, Merton often uses the word *depressed* to describe himself. In his journal Merton is free to be himself, but those portions of his private journals that he published were finely crafted *before* publication. Merton's journals had also to pass the censors—the Imprimatur, the Imprimi Potest, the Nihil Obstat—and he was ever aware of his Catholic persona and his Catholic readers.

Speaking of persona, Merton is intrigued by the personae he has created during his life. Still reeling from Zilboorg's excoriation, he wrote in his journal entry of August 26, 1956, about receiving a letter from an imaginary character named Tranche-Chef:

> I am again wondering how to think of myself as an artist. Strange, that an actor like myself, should be dominated by a fantasy of myself as a very modest person. Sincerely, it rarely, if ever occurs to me that I might be vain or proud. Am I really a proud man?

And yet it seems I have actually believed myself to be all the characters I have portrayed. It is as if in exhibiting myself to the world in an endless variety of roles, I were saying (in my modesty) "You see I am all those but much more too for the real 'I' transcends them all and gives them all life." Now tell me, is this really pride. Or is it not after all a modesty or unimpeachable innocence? [19]

There is a poignancy of pathos to the above passage because, if anything, it proves that Zilboorg hit a nerve with Merton, and for better or worse, Merton wonders if there could have been any truth to the remarks tossed at him by Zilboorg. The key to understanding the passage is Merton's admission that he is indeed an actor, which is indicative of the fact that Merton is well aware of the various personae he has worn over the years and still wears. To employ his own language, he recognized and knows his false selves (Mott says Merton had employed over *fifty* alter egos in his writing.)[20]

Zilboorg, on the other hand, actually has been an actor on stage. The question Merton should have asked him (had he not broken down weeping) would be, "Do *you* know when you are acting and when you are not?" A proud and vain man often believes in his masks, and sometimes he is not even aware that he is wearing them. An honest man is aware, and it is this very honesty that renders him modest. True modesty is in touch with the true "I."

# Melancholy, Another Code Word for Depression?

## The Anatomy of Melancholy
There was a man, born like
Other men, but he had a
Different name. He always

Took himself seriously
And kept his head before it was too late,
Because his nurse had
Struck him in the cradle.

Wherever he went he kept his
Eye on the clock. His heart was not
On his sleeve, but his tongue was ready
With a civil answer.

One day he could not find his feet.
He lost his balance and began to sing.
When he sang, they paid him to shut up,
He was no longer happy when he smiled.

He tried to walk and they
Put him in jail. He spoke
And showed a broken tooth.
When he sat down he lost face.

It was a long night before he woke up
And he was found beside himself when he
Came to his senses.
No one cared to have him around
Though his heart was in the right place
Clucking like a hen.

No one remembered but the business men
Who entered brandishing a bill.
They greeted him and smiled as they sat.
"You have," they said, (as he lost his voice)
"A serious problem."
So they took away his house.

The cops went off
With his sister and daughter.
He kept a stiff upper lip but no
Money and no social standing.

"What shall I do?" he cried, "drink or gamble?"
He left in no direction, followed by his dog
(the dog is man's best friend), and

Puritans had them arrested
For romping as they walked
And barking as they spoke.[21]

"The Anatomy of Melancholy" is best read as an autobiographical/confessional poem. The first draft appears in his journal entry of September 1, 1956, after Merton has attended a conference at St. John's University in Collegeville, Minnesota, where psychiatrist Gregory Zilboorg was the keynote presenter. Merton is enmeshed in another of a continuing series of sporadic stability crises, begging his abbot for more solitude, hoping to be allowed to become a true hermit. Abbot Fox attends the very same conference, arriving at its conclusion. It is a tense time for Merton, when, Monica Furlong observes, Merton "teetered on the edge of a breakdown."[22]

Before Merton writes "Melancholy," he engages in a prewriting journal exercise on September 1, 1956, to answer a question from an imaginary character Merton names Tranche-Chef: "Let us walk along here," said Tranche-Chef "And compose a number of sentences each one of which begins with the words 'You think you are a monk but....'" Tranche-Chef interrupts, "But what are you doing?" The following is his answer:

**Exercise**

Is there any law to forbid
Inventing a person? Or is every
Creature of the mind another self?
Is not one self enough? Is it
Pride to make more of them?
To populate a whole world with
Oneself—I mean, of course, in a
Novel. In a word, I ask—
Show me why I
Should feel, as I do feel,
Guilty when I invent a person?[23]

Merton is by nature a writer, but from March 1953 to July 1956, he was forbidden by Dom Sortais to write in his journal. It is while writing in his journal that Merton is able to explore himself, to tackle head-on pressing personal issues. It is a vital outlet in his individuation process. As a monk, he is dedicated to unveiling the false selves he has created during his life; only by constant vigilance has he become aware of the various masks he used. Wearing personae (masks), however, is not dangerous for the man who is *aware* of them.

His first abbot had permitted Merton to wear the mask of writer, as a Catholic apologist at the forefront of Catholic spiritual writing, up there with other well-known Catholic writers like Bishop Fulton J. Sheen. It so happened that Merton's "writer's mask" became as famous as Sheen's. Although he made a great amount of money for the Abbey of Gethsemani, Merton, having taken a vow of poverty, had no personal bank account for his royalties. It all went into the abbey's coffers.

For Merton, the mask of writer is closer to who he really is than any other mask, perhaps closer than the mask of monk and priest. Writers are born with their talent, monks and priests are called by God. There is a difference between being born with genius and being called to the Religious life. Because Merton's abbots allow him to write, he is able to combine various masks: monk, priest, writer, correspondent, essayist, poet, spiritual director. But the combination often creates much conflict and guilt. It should be noted that by allowing Merton to write, Abbot Dunne violated the strictest sense of the Rule of St. Benedict. His motive may have been a monetary one, for the abbey was on the brink of financial ruin, and Merton's writing was a possible financial solution to the problem, as it indeed proved to be: Merton's royalties were substantial. So Abbot Fox continued to allow Merton to write—except for the ban in the early 1950s when the orders of Dom Sortais forbade Merton to keep his journal.

In his "Exercise," Merton asks, "Is there any law to forbid / Inventing a person? Or is every / creature of the mind another self?" He asks this question while he is also composing "The Anatomy of Melancholy." When an author writes, he can only create from his own life's experience. Thus, in analyzing this poem, the reader is not reckless to assume that Merton is writing about himself.

In "The Anatomy of Melancholy," Merton creates a mask for himself. To understand the poem and to penetrate its mystery, it is best to treat the poem as a riddle, for it is fraught with references to Merton's life.

Merton employs the Victorian word for depression, *melancholy*, to distance himself from it. In times past, people were ashamed to admit that they suffered from depression. The late writer William Styron, who wrote *Darkness Visible*, a best-selling account about his depression and flirtation with suicide, avoided using the word *depression*, also preferring the word *melancholy*.

By using *anatomy*, Merton incarnates melancholy so that he (and we) can "see" and perhaps better understand it. Instead of "Once upon a time there was a man," the traditional opening of a fairly tale, Merton begins, "There was a man." The man is born like any other man, but he has a different name from Merton's; in other words, Merton implies that the poem is not about "me." Like most men, he takes himself seriously—the ego strengthens and grows as one matures from childhood. There is a reference to an early childhood wound inflicted by his nurse: "Because his nurse had / Struck him in the cradle." This could be an oblique reference to the severity of Merton's mother (the original cause of his depression?). Or it could perhaps be a reference to his brother's birth when his mother seemingly rejected Tom to focus on the new baby, John Paul.

The man grew up, but "His heart was not / On his sleeve." Here we have an accurate description of Merton in regard to women and to love. He was a man afraid to reveal his vulnerability, to show love and to accept love. Thus, his inability ever to form a lasting relationship with a woman continued. He was still a popular man, however, still socializing and dating, always "ready with a civil answer."

Then occurs a sudden loss: "One day he could not find his feet." Feet allow us to stand firmly, they ground us. He loses "his balance." Depression is often sudden and swiftly floors its victim. When the subject begins to sing, "they paid him to shut up." One remembers Merton's falling in the sanctuary while intoning Mass, which happened shortly after his ordination, the time of his breakdown. If we accept this interpretation, then the verse, "When he sat down he lost face," could refer to Merton's utter shame from fainting. "To shut up" could be a reference to the ongoing trouble he had with the order's censors. The mention of the "broken tooth" could also be a self-reference; Merton had constant trouble with his teeth, and the pain often resulted in depression. (This leitmotif permeates almost all of the many novels of Merton's contemporary, Graham Greene, a Catholic convert like Merton.)

His autobiography records several accounts of trouble with his teeth, and at one point he was very ill with both an infected toe and tooth. The tooth had to be extracted: "And I heard them [school doctor and Dr. McTaggart] agreeing that I was too full of gangrene for my own good. They decided to lance a big hole in my gum, and see if they could not drain the pocket of infection there and so, having given me a little ether, they went ahead. I awoke with my mouth full of filth."[24]

When the man finally "Came to his senses," he realizes that no one wants to have him around; he feels bad about it because "his heart was in the right place": He wanted to be liked and understood. Merton, too, wanted to be liked and accepted by his community even though he was often quite critical of it.

Then the "business men" arrive "brandishing a bill." They smilingly greet the man, seemingly friendly. They, however, tell him he has a "serious problem"; consequently, he loses everything, including his family, and is left with nothing: no "money, and no social standing." And they "took away his house," which is likely a reference to Merton's departing England forever at the suggestion of his guardian Tom Bennett after Merton had sired an illegitimate child.

This situation can happen to the chronically depressed (melancholic). If their depression is serious enough, they may be institutionalized, and thus they "lose" everything. Here the man ends up alone, except for the presence of his dog, "man's best friend." The dog is likely a reminder of young Tom's childhood imaginary dog, Doolittle.

How else may we apply the poem to Merton's life? His abbot thought he, indeed, suffered serious psychological problems and, as mentioned above, allowed him to meet the well-known psychiatrist Gregory Zilboorg, who had actually said Merton had a "serious problem."

In the poem, the man's adversary is "business men." Abbot Fox was a graduate of Harvard Business School, and himself an astute businessman. Had he "hired" Zilboorg in his attempt to keep Merton at Gethsemani? Merton's biographer Michael Mott doubts the idea that the meeting between Merton and Zilboorg was a trap or setup, but it is still a distinct possibility. Even Merton, in a 1959 journal entry, states his belief that Abbot Fox had used "a couple of wild remarks by Zilboorg that I was likely to take off with a woman and leave the church, etc." against him with the Congregation of the Religious, comments that likely kept Merton from ever transferring to another abbey or religious order.[25]

Or could the reference to a "bill" concern the financial settlement Tom Bennett brokered when Tom fathered a child out of wedlock? Thus, Bennett could also be considered either one of the businessmen of the poem or perhaps one of the "cops" who "went off with his sister and daughter." Could this line be Merton's oblique reference (by reversing roles and gender) to the mother ("sister") and child ("daughter") he was "relieved of"? Could he have been urged by Tom Bennett to face his problem like a man "with a stiff upper lip"? Such an abandonment of mother and child and a financial settlement, by the way, would leave him alone, without "money and no social standing." Bennett had informed the young Merton that fathering a child out of wedlock eliminated his chance of a career in the British Civil Service, and Bennett encouraged him to remain in America (Merton's antipathy for England he later regretted, for he also had happy memories of England, of staying with his Aunt Maud and of being a student at Oakham).

The last stanza of the poem says, "Puritans had them arrested." We do not think it far-fetched to consider this reference to the censors who often tried to "arrest" his writing, that is, stop it. Censors were an ongoing problem during Merton's monastic life. Arresting Puritans may also refer to both Fox and Zilboorg, Fox for stopping Merton's transfer from Gethsemani, and Zilboorg for warning Merton not to publish his article on

"Neurosis in the Monastery." (The latter was reworked and posthumously published in the 1991 *Merton Annual*.)

Of course, we can only speculate about how much this poem truly and accurately mirrors Merton's life, but melancholy (depression) was surely on Merton's mind, particularly in the mid-1950s; the poem's existence is proof enough. Writing had always been an outlet for Merton, and since he was banned from writing his journal, composing poems became a saving grace when he was obsessed with seeking more solitude in another community. Poetry became his "medicine." (He resumed his journal on July 17, 1956. Some of the poems of *The Strange Islands* had already been composed, for example, "Elias" in late 1954; "The Anatomy of Melancholy" was composed in September of 1956 after "Whether There Is Enjoyment in Bitterness," which was composed in late July 1956).

At the time of the composition of "Melancholy," Merton writes, "On the surface I have my confusion. On a deeper level, desire and conflict. In the greatest depths, like a spring of pure water rising up in the flames of hell, is the smallness, the frailty of hope that is, yet never overwhelmed but continues strangely and inexplicably to nourish in the midst of apparent despair."[26]

Caught in "apparent despair," Merton continues to pray, however, and it helps him to take one step at a time so that if he falls from a precipice, it is more like a leap of prayer. Such is his hope against "the emptiness and helplessness and humiliation. Aware that I might crack up at any moment. I find, nevertheless, that when I pray, I pray better than ever."[27]

There are two other poems that reveal Merton's emotional supersensitivity. He was exquisitely attuned to sound; thus, the guns of Fort Knox were a constant irritation to him as well as the proliferation of the noise of machines at Gethsemani, still a working farm. Two poems in *The Strange Islands* address this issue: "The Guns of Fort Knox" and "Exploits of a Machine Age."

Merton dreamed of an (admittedly fantastical) abbey where absolute silence prevailed.

Artists are, of course, "different" from ordinary people. If certain conditions are not met, it is difficult for them to create. It is astounding that Merton, even though he was plagued by a number of issues at Gethsemani, including his psychological problems, produced an enormous corpus of work. In fact, his output is staggering when one views the number of books, articles, and poems he wrote, often composed when he was either physically or psychologically unwell. It is even more astounding when one factors in the hours devoted to prayer each day: Vigils, Matins, Lauds, Prime, Terce, Sext, None, Vespers, and Compline, along with *daily* Holy Mass, recitation of the rosary, lectio divina—*and*, on top of all this spiritual activity, hours of manual labor. As the Rule of St. Benedict reads: "Ora et Labora."

# Chapter Eight

The years after the notorious Zilboorg affair, and before Merton's falling in love with his nurse in March of 1966, are ones of self-discovery as well as time fraught with old longings and complaints nagging at him. If we chart his journey, therefore, we find many highs and many lows. If Merton penned a wish list, it would likely include his perennial yearnings: a hermitage, peace with the censors, more solitude, more silence, more prayer, among others. His dream of a hermitage would likely appear at the top of his list.

In February of 1953, Merton receives permission to spend time in an old, abandoned toolshed, a hermitage he names in honor of St. Anne. It is a place that offers him a taste of what greater silence and solitude would mean; he writes, "St. Anne's is like a rampart between two existences. On one side I know the community to which I must return. And I can return to it with love. But to return seems like a waste. It is a waste I offer to God. On the other side is the great wilderness of silence in which, perhaps, I might never speak to anyone but God again, as long as I live....It seems to me that St. Anne's is what I have been waiting for and looking for all my life and I have stumbled into it quite by accident. Now, for the first time, I am aware of what happens to a man who has really found his place in the scheme of things."[1]

Later, a hermitage within the grounds of Gethsemani proves to be insufficient when Merton's stability crisis again raises its head. Merton shares his desire to leave Gethsemani with the poet

Ernesto Cardenal, a former novice at Gethsemani who encourages Merton to leave Kentucky.

Cardenal spurs Merton's interest in South America and its poets. Merton also wants to know more about Russia and is enamored of Pasternak's novel *Doctor Zhivago*, writing two studies of it, both of which Pasternak reads and approves. He continues his study of Zen, and he continues to write poetry.

Sometimes his goals are grandiose; he writes:

> If I can unite *in myself*, in my own spiritual life, the thought of the East and the West of the Greek and Latin Fathers, I will create in myself a reunion of the divided church and from that unity in myself can come the exterior and visible unity of the Church. For if we want to bring together the East and West we cannot do it by imposing one upon the other. We must contain both in ourselves and transcend both in Christ.[2]

His idealism is obviously still intact as well as his growing concern about the many divisions in the world. He fears that there may be another war capable of destroying the world with which he has only lately fallen in love. He is also obliquely referring to the divisions within himself, particularly his opposition to Abbot Fox, who, he fears (correctly), worked against his move from Gethsemani to a hermitage elsewhere.

The year 1958 is important for Merton. It is the year of his dream of Proverb, in which a young Jewish girl embraces Merton. Later, he composes his now famous Proverb letters, illustrating his efforts to come to terms with his anima.

> Dear Proverb,
> And in you dear, though some might be tempted to say you do not even exist, there is a reality as real and

as wonderful and as precious as life itself. I must be careful what I say, for words cannot explain my love for you, and I do not wish, by my words, to harm that which in you is more real and more pure than in anyone else in the world—your lovely spontaneity, your simplicity, the generosity of your love.[3]

Soon after there follows his Louisville Vision, recorded on March 19, 1958, laying to rest forever any residual *contemptus mundi* that may have lingered in Merton's soul. Merton credits Proverb with his Louisville Vision: "I shall never forget our meeting yesterday. The touch of your hand makes me a different person. To be with you is rest and truth. Only with you are these things found, dear child sent to me by God."[4] After it, Merton becomes more passionately interested in people, in current affairs, particularly the Cold War, world peace, Civil Rights, and in the 1960s, the war in Vietnam. After many years of intense introspection, he again considers himself a member of the human race.

In 1958, he publishes *Thoughts in Solitude*, one of his wisest books. In 1959, after much wrangling over who owned the copyright and confrontations with the censors, he sees the publication of *The Secular Journal of Thomas Merton* as well as his *Selected Poems*. *The New Man* came out in 1961; his controversial *Original Child Bomb* appears in 1962. In the latter, Merton questions America's dropping the atomic bomb on Japan at the end of World War II. He is now unafraid to enter dangerous political waters; if he is to be of use to the world as a marginal man (his description of himself), he must have the courage of his convictions, and the courage to express them. Merton has developed a horror of being inauthentic, nearly obsessed with the idea of the false and the True Self. He strives always to discover his True Self, a pursuit which often causes him much pain. Many of

America's bishops as well as a goodly number of Merton's readers feel that he should not be commenting on political issues, that he should keep writing his small, spiritually uplifting books like *No Man Is an Island*, but he ignores them.

In the late fifties, Merton still feels he is called to a life of greater solitude. A few bishops invite him to their dioceses to establish himself as a hermit, places like San Juan, and Eureka, Nevada. Ernesto Cardenal suggests a group of islands off the coast of Nicaragua. Dom Gregorio Lemercier, the prior of Our Lady of the Resurrection of Cuernavaca, also invites him. But Merton cannot make up his mind, although at one point it looks as if he favors going to Mexico.

What is Merton looking for exactly? In a journal entry for July 23, 1958, Merton outlines his idea for an ideal monastery; it reveals much about why he so seriously considers leaving Gethsemani.

A small monastery.

1. Without a "program."
2. Without a special job to do. Monks to *live*, not to be "monks" as distinct from every other kind of being, but to be *men*—sons of God.
3. Without special future. No drive for postulants.
4. Without a special reputation or renown for anything.
5. A hidden monastery, not well known, perhaps a monastery. Perhaps not even wearing a special habit. Without observably distinctive buildings.
6. But certainly isolated, cloistered and cut off.
7. With hermit types—i.e. possibilities for personal solitude for a certain portion of the year. Special solitude in certain seasons. Advent, Lent.
8. Made up of a nucleus of *mature* monks, each one able to decide for himself in fasting, etc.

9. Taking an interest in art, music, Literature, politics, etc. of our time.

10. Manual Labor of course. Maybe some teaching. *But care to keep the life from getting crowded with works and projects.*[5]

[Emphases in original]

He still follows the Rule of St. Benedict and the *Horae Canonicae*. It is an intriguing summary of what actually constitutes an ideal monastery; in fact, what Merton has given us is his version of a monastic Utopia. It also informs us, albeit obliquely, of what is "wrong" with Gethsemani. During Advent of the same year, however, Merton paradoxically writes:

I am here (at Gethsemani) gratis, for no special purpose, with no strings attached, freely. I have no serious reason for wanting to be elsewhere, though I might like to be elsewhere at times. The fact remains that elsewhere is not where I am, or where I am likely to be. The point is not that this is a sublimely wonderful and special place. Not at all. To try to convince myself of this after 17 years would be madness and insincerity. The point is that it does not much matter where you are, as long as you can be at peace about it and live your life. The place certainly will not live my life for me, I have found that out. I have to live it for myself.[6]

In June of the following year, however, he is still interested in going to a "small semi-eremitical community" located on the Corn Islands off Nicaragua. If not there, he still hopes to have a hermitage on the grounds of Gethsemani (the toolshed proves insufficient). But his worrying about where to go has by now reached the crisis stage: "The great problem in this crisis is to keep from going from one fiction to another: from the communal fiction which we cherish as a group, to a private fiction which I cherish as an individual." His anxiety had a psychological impact: "This vocation business is making me miserable."[7]

On July 2, 1959, he records in his journal that "the time has come for me to leave."[8] To understand why he wanted to leave Gethsemani, he lists his negative motives for remaining:

- you are here, can't get out so don't try
- what will people think?
- you have a life you can easily live here—it is safe and secure. Why take a risk?
- you are content here—You will always be respected and influential in the community and in the U.S. Is this not God's will?
- it is easy to write books here—you can get all the books you want too…etc.
- and you love the novices. They are a kind of family to you, aren't they?[9]

He discusses his problem with Abbot Fox, who advises him that if remaining at Gethsemani is a sacrifice, then it is good because suffering would sanctify him. Merton is not convinced, concluding, "To say here is no real sacrifice, no progress, no real virtue, only inertia, acceptance of mediocrity."[10] In a more emotional entry, after a talk with Abbot Fox, Merton seemingly quotes him: "Hence, life at Gethsemani is a 'perpetual martyrdom.' 'It costs, it costs.' It is like being 'boiled in oil.'"[11]

In mid-July, Merton learns that Abbot Fox is to go to Rome. He is certain it has something to do with his request for a transfer. In the meantime, he is busy writing *The Inner Experience* and reading Massignon's *Seven Sleepers* and Mark van Doren's *Poetry as Knowledge*. He discovers the mystics of the fourteenth century, for example, Rolle, *The Cloud of Unknowing*, and Lady Julian of Norwich. Of the fourteenth century, he writes, "It is my own century, the one whose spirit is most mine."[12]

On November 19, he lists his goals:

1. I really want to live alone in simplicity and devote myself to thought and prayer.
2. No *typewriter*.
3. Strictly selected books—about 100. Especially hope to work on Philokalia.
4. Renounce all *comfort*, the *reputation*, the *security*, the American friendships which bind me here and make me part of the collective falsity and injustice of this society.
5. Renounce this kind of cenobitism.[13]

The end of 1959 is a dark time for Merton. There is no sign of any solution to his stability crisis. True to his surname, Abbot Fox plays a foxy game with Merton, denying him some of his mail. Merton confesses to understanding for the first time the psalm "about the temptation to despair that beset the poor and oppressed. They wanted the right words to pour balm in certain wounds."[14]

When the long-awaited letter about Merton's request to live a hermit's life (either at Gethsemani or elsewhere) arrives from Rome, Fox quickly hands this letter over to him. Signed by two cardinals, it declares that Merton "did not have an eremitical vocation. That therefore what they asked of me was to stay in the monastery where God had put me, and I would find interior solitude."[15]

He seemingly accepts their decision as God's will for him, but he feels betrayed and requests for and receives permission for sessions with Dr. Wygal in Louisville. He is convinced that Zilboorg's wild remarks about taking off with a woman and leaving the church were used by Abbot Fox in Rome. He thinks that he should find out if he, indeed, suffers from neurotic instability, although he doubts it. And if Wygal can prove there is no danger for Merton to being out on his own, Rome may revise its decision.

Merton takes stock of his situation at Gethsemani:

1. I still believe this is not really the "right place" for me…
2. I am fully able to accept, and have accepted the decision that I should stay here…
3. I do not feel that it is for me to take any positive initiative, except to make known that my desires are still the same.
4. And also declare that should the Bishop or someone present a strong argument in my favor and if the opinion of the Sacred Congregation change I would be willing to accept an indult and make a trial of a different life at Cuernavaca.[16]

Merton, soon after composing this list, questions whether he has the right to make judgments about his life or anyone else's life:

Is it a temptation for me to want to form judgments and enumerate them, judgments about the situation of many today? Sometimes I imagine that this is pride and megalomania—as if I were an authority. Who am I? The point is that I have acquired the power to be heard, and there is every evidence that I should use it discreetly and modestly, when it seems that I have something to say. The humble and prudent solution is then to accept the responsibilities this entails, to mistrust my own observations and limitations but to study and think and, when opportune or fitting, to speak. There is no megalomania in this if I don't delude myself that I am a prophet or a doctor of the church.[17]

The use of the word *megalomania* brings to mind Zilboorg's scathing attack on Merton in 1956.

During Merton's life, rumors that he would eventually leave Gethsemani never cease. On December 26, 1960, he is daily allowed to stay for hours at the new cinderblock hermitage, named after St. Mary of Carmel (the new recipient of his anima projection, explained below). He writes:

But St. Mary of Carmel (after Vespers) this is tremendous: with the tall pines, the silence, the moon and stars above the pines as dark falls, the patterns of shadow, the vast valley and hills everything speaks of a more mature and more complete solitude. The pines are tall and not low. There is frankly a house, demanding not attachment but responsibility. A silence for dedication and not for escape. Lit candles in the dusk. *Haec requies mea in saculum saculi* (This is my resting place forever)—the sense of a journey ended, of wandering at an end. The first time in my life I ever really felt I had come home and that my waiting and looking were ended.[18]

Merton is happy. It has taken him a long time to feel that he "had come home." But having a hermitage does not solve all his problems with his abbot or with the abbey. He and Abbot Fox are both wary of each other. Merton suspects that Fox had abused his power and enjoys teasing him about his mail. A letter from Ernesto Cardenal, marked "Conscience Matter," Fox quickly returns to Cardenal. Merton argues that Cardenal is a close friend, but Fox is unmoved. Merton writes:

> At that moment I could see Dom James's expression. He was triumphant. To say that I had an intimate friend was quite simply to acknowledge a particular friendship. How happy he was. He was totally vindicated. I was a homosexual....You see how he makes his judgments. And because of the reasons given by this kind of superior, the Sacred Congregation has thrown out my application.[19]

Merton is also having trouble with the abbot general, Gabriel Sortais, who denies Merton's request to include an introduction to *The Wisdom of the Desert* by Daisetz Teitaro Suzuki. Sortais's objections to another of Merton's books, *Disputed Questions*, holds up the publication of the book. In the former, a Zen scholar and a Christian monk discuss connections between the sayings of Zen monks and those of the desert fathers. In the latter, Merton is frankly critical of his order. These publication problems occur a year or two before the ecumenical council when most of Sortais's objections would become moot, but it surely must have been frustrating for Merton to have to face so much opposition from his superiors, a price he has to pay for being light years ahead of his time.

His problems with the powers-that-be, however, do not dampen his curiosity. His interest in so many things continues to burgeon: in photography, the Shakers, Italian architecture, Russian literature, Chinese, and calligraphy. He also maintains a correspondence with a number of people, the most enriching perhaps that with Czeslaw Milosz, the Polish writer who would one day win the Nobel Prize.

These two men are kindred spirits. They have battled stifling authoritarianism much of their adult lives, although Merton's may be said to be on a microcosmic level: his abbot, his abbot general, and the order's censors, while Milosz's is on a macrocosmic one: communism. Milosz opens Merton's eyes to many things; he also inspires him to read Simone Weil and encourages him to read the poet Robinson Jeffers and the Greek poet Constantine Cavafy. They do not see, however, eye to eye on everything. For example, Milosz does not particularly like Merton's poetry (nor does T. S. Eliot). The Polish writer also criticizes Merton as being too romantic about nature, but he admires Merton's book *Thoughts in Solitude*, a book of reflections that has held up well and is still in print.

During this time, Merton is also working on his "renderings" from the Chinese as well as his prose poem "Hagia Sophia," one of his most beautiful works, which his friend Victor Hammer publishes in a magnificent limited edition. In addition, Merton sees the publication of *A Thomas Merton Reader* (edited by Thomas P. McDonnell) and his revised early book, now called *New Seeds of Contemplation*. The latter is an expanded and wiser book, minus the *contemptus mundi* that marred the first *Seeds*. By the time he has revised *Seeds*, Merton, well versed in Carl Jung's theory and under the influence of Jung's papers from the *Eranos Yearbooks*, is now quoting him:

> People will do anything, no matter how absurd, to avoid facing their own psyches. All because they cannot get on with themselves and *have not the slightest faith that anything useful could ever come out of the psyche*. [Merton's emphasis] August 11, 1962[20]

In October of 1962, Merton describes himself and his time:

> Though I am nearly 48, and it is doubtless time to feel
> a change of climate in my physical being, which
> begins to dispose itself for its end some one of these
> years, it is useless to interpret every little sign or sug-
> gestion of change as something of significance....My
> impatience is felt as an upheaval of resentment, dis-
> gust, depression....The colossal sense of failure in the
> midst of success, that is characteristic of America.[21]

By the time Christmas of 1962 arrives, Merton falls into his
usual Christmas depression. Thinking about the practice of
exchanging Christmas gifts, Merton records this seeming non
sequitur:

> I saw the connection with my own life, and my fail-
> ure to really trust another person enough to give
> myself completely to her. My sexual adventures were
> always seductions—I wanted them to be conquests,
> in which in reality I gave nothing, only "took." But I
> believe my need, and perhaps my latent capacity to
> give myself was once very deep. Now—well, I get
> depressed. I remember the frequency of Christmas
> depressions in the past few years, and have come to
> expect them as a matter of course.[22]

He admits, however, that his first Christmas at Gethsemani
was "fantastically pure and happy." Such happiness, he confesses, remains in the depths of his soul. Has it, however, become
merely a happy memory? Here we should state that when the
ego is out of touch with its anima or animus, the person often

becomes a lost soul, for the soul is the connecting mechanism that offers life meaning.

The soul image can be projected onto things and people. Merton as a celibate monk cannot "attach" himself to the opposite sex. The substitute is the Abbey of Our Lady of Gethsemani. What happens if what the soul image has attached itself to loses her luster? Or in other words, she has fallen out of love? James Hall writes:

> The soul image gives a sense of meaningful connection beyond oneself, or at least the possibility of such connection. It is a sense of direction, intimately concerned with the individuation process. Like all senses, it can be mistaken in its goal and it can miscarry.[23]

On many occasions, Merton, indeed, sounds like a lost soul. His anima projection onto the Abbey of Gethsemani and Mother Church once made him happy, but one can only be happy if one believes one's projection is accepted and treasured. Merton has been attacked on many fronts: on his desire to transfer, on being a hermit, on his views on peace, war, nuclear arms, and even on his innocent friendships, for example, Ernesto Cardenal. He is in desperate need of a new recipient for his anima projection since Gethsemani has become too critical of him. A temporary solution turns out to be his new hermitage, but it also loses its attraction, and he finds himself projecting his anima onto a woman (more later).

In 1963, Merton published *Breakthrough to Peace, Life and Holiness* and *Emblems of a Season of Fury*. The latter is a mixed bag of poems. There are poems of anger, elegies, and several very fine poems about the spiritual life: the exquisite lyrics "Song for Nobody," "Night-Flowering Cactus," "Love Winter When the Plant Says Nothing," and "Hagia Sophia."

In a May 1963 journal entry, Merton examines himself:

Today is the fourteenth anniversary of my ordination
to the priesthood. I wish I could say they had been
fourteen years of ever-growing fulfillment and order
and integration. That is unfortunately not so. They
have been years of relative happiness and productiv-
ity on the surface, but now I realize more and more
the depth of my frustration and the apparent finality
of my defeat. I have certainly not fitted into the con-
ventional—or even traditional—mold....I have a very
real sense that it has all been some kind of lie, a cha-
rade. With all my blundering attempts at sincerity I
have actually done nothing to change this....Probably
the chief weakness has been lack of real courage to
bear up under the attrition of monastic and priestly
life. Anyway, I am worn down. I am easily discour-
aged. The depressions are deeper, more frequent. I
am near fifty. People think I am happy.[24]

It is poignantly sad that Merton feels so negatively about
himself. He has become a leading voice in the Catholic Church.
His books (translated into many languages) are read by a wide
spectrum of readers, both Catholic and non-Catholic. He has
helped to transform people's lives by his insights into the contemplative life, and although Fox does not acknowledge it (to
Merton's face), he exerts a great impact on monastic life at
Gethsemani; yet on the whole, he feels like a defeated man. Part
of the problem is similar to the one many teachers must feel:
When they see their students leave, they do not know the extent
of their influence. A doctor has immediate feedback: The operation is a success or an ill patient is now cured. An engineer sees
his new building standing before him. The lawyer hears whether

or not he has won or lost a case. Merton never really understands the tremendous impact his writing has exerted on the world. With Abbot Fox, it is always a game of chess, one of them trying to outmaneuver the other, but the game is fixed in the abbot's favor; Abbot Fox possesses both influence and power in America and in Rome.

Merton records the following dream on October 6, 1963:

> Dreamt last night of Italian Cathedrals (not real ones, dream ones). First I am with others of the community in a crowded Cathedral at "Siena." Confusion. I am trying to pray, turned toward a stonelike tabernacle beyond the crowd. (Is it the tabernacle?) I think of going to the "Shrine of St. Catherine." Then I am in another spacious well-lighted Cathedral "nearer home" and I am trying to "remember" the name of the city which should be very familiar. (Mantua?) I am struck and appeased by the airiness and spaciousness of the cathedral, the high shadowy vaults with paintings. A Nazareth nun walks through the cathedral and I am afraid she will recognize me. I pray. I cannot remember the name of the place where I am, a city perhaps beginning with "C." Or "Mantua" perhaps? But no, Mantua is in the "North of Italy" and I am more in the center.[25]

The dream mirrors Merton's stability crisis. The cathedral is too crowded and this crowdedness affects his "trying to pray" (we remember his unsuccessful attempt to pray as a youth in a European church in *The Seven Storey Mountain*). Gethsemani was an overcrowded and noisy place, not conducive to contemplation. He decides to leave this cathedral for another (as he wanted to leave Gethsemani for another order); he finds himself in a place "well-lighted" and "nearer home." *Home* is the pivotal word: We are left to speculate on what was home to Merton. This cathedral aesthetically impresses him; it contains "shadowy vaults with paintings." But his appeasement is then threatened when a "Nazareth nun walks through the cathedral." This is an allusion to his anima problem, his "refusal of woman," one yet to be solved. He becomes confused and does not know where he is; he is sure he is not in the "North of Italy" but in the center. The word *center* is important. According to Jung, the center of the psyche is the Self; Merton is, indeed, moving toward his center, toward his True Self, but he still has more soul work to do, primarily facing and addressing the nun within him, the nun who frightens him, his anima.

Again in February 1964, Merton offers another evaluation of his life:

> Today is the twenty-second anniversary of my reception of the habit. And in all sobriety and honesty I must admit that the twenty-two years have not been well spent, at least as far as my part in them has been concerned, although from God there has been nothing but grace and mercy. Rather twenty-two years of relative confusion, often coming close to doubt and infidelity, agonized aspirations for "something better," criticism of what I have, inexplicable inner suffering that is largely my own fault, insufficient efforts to overcome myself, inability to find my way, perhaps culpably straying off into things that do not concern me....I do know this—that after the first half year or (beginner's consolation!) I ran into years of false fervor, asceticism, intransigence, intolerance, and this lasted more or less until I was ordained.[26]

When one reads this entry, one wants to reread his journal entries about his first years at Gethsemani. It is surprising to find that volume 1 of Merton's Journals covers only these dates: December 1941–April 1942, followed by a several years' gap and then resumed, in December 1946. The years from 1943 to 1946 are not covered. Merton tore up his journal, a very unusual act for Merton, who found it difficult to destroy any of his writing; he made sure he kept his pre-Gethsemani writing, especially his poetry and his novels. Thus, we will never know the length and depth of his first monastic journal; he sent its remnants to Sister Therese Lentfoehr, a mere eleven pages of his "Novitiate Journal." Why did he destroy it? What did it contain? Would it have shed light on the passage just quoted?

We are thankful to have his "The Whale and the Ivy Journal," from which he extracted his popular *The Sign of Jonas*. What a terrible loss it would have been had he destroyed it.

In June of 1964, when he learns that Suzuki is to be staying in New York, Merton fears it will likely be his last chance to meet the great Zen scholar who is now ninety-four and frail. Merton has long admired Suzuki, has read and studied his work and discovered affinities between Western and Eastern contemplation. Dom Fox reluctantly agrees to Merton's visiting Suzuki and parcels out to him just enough money to cover basic expenses (how ironic that Merton, who made so much money for Gethsemani, was given so little for his traveling expenses). The New York visit is one of the highlights of Merton's life.

When he arrives, he finds a far different New York, not the one he left just as World War II was to begin. There is a new tension in the air, but he appreciatively walks the city, sleeping at Butler Hall, Columbia, his alma mater, and celebrating Mass alone at Corpus Christi where he was baptized a Catholic.

His two long talks with Suzuki are a success:

These talks were very pleasant, and profoundly important to me—to see and experience the fact that there
really is a deep understanding between myself and this
extraordinary and simple man whom I have been reading for about ten years with great attention.[27]

He is amazed at how at home he feels with Suzuki and his
secretary Mihoko Okamura, feeling as comfortable with them as
he felt with Victor Hammer and his wife. Suzuki also compli-
ments him on one of his Zen essays, "one of the best things on
Zen to have been written in the West." Merton, along with Alan
Watts, was a leading intellectual able to write knowledgeably
and insightfully about Zen and its practice and its potential con-
gruence with Christianity. At the time, many Catholics did not
understand (and some still do not) Merton's interest in Zen. For
a glimpse into his interest, one need only read his essay, "A
Christian looks at Zen":

Buddhist meditation, but above all that of Zen, seeks
not *to explain* but *to pay attention, to become aware, to
be mindful,* in other words to develop *a certain kind of
consciousness that is above and beyond deception* by ver-
bal formulas—or by emotional excitement.[28]

On August 12, 1964, Merton records the following dream:

Last night I dreamed that Dom James suddenly
announced that we would have funeral and quasi-
military "parades for the dead" along with every
Office of the Dead from now on. Monks would march
in spaced ranks, slowly through the church for a long

> time. I saw this begin and saw that the sick were all forced to participate. Even the dead were in it, for Father Alphonsus was there, albeit stumbling. The Abbot was absolutely insistent on this preposterous new observance, as a firm manifestation of his will. I tried to reason with him, on the grounds of "simplicity," and even tried to find a copy of *The Spirit of Simplicity* for him to read but could find none.[29]

The dream reflects Merton's feeling about his abbot: Fox is militaristic, dictatorial, irrational, inflexible, and preposterous (absurd). Merton sees him as a man who espouses a Catholicism that was quickly dying, thus the "parades for the dead"—the abbot, however, does not understand what or who is currently dying: It was a time of *aggiornamento*, which literally means to bring up to date. The abbot seems not to understand for whom the bell tolls, for if he did, he would have ordered celebrations not of the dead but of the living, called for rites not of death but those of joy and rejoicing. The time when monks marched strictly in "spaced ranks" was over, and for Merton it was about time.

Merton searches in vain for the book he wrote (although his name as author does not appear): *The Spirit of Simplicity*. The unspoken question to his abbot seems to be, "Why do you make everything so complicated, when in fact it is quite simple?"

To Merton's surprise Abbot Fox, in real life, is changing his views of solitude; Merton's ideas are, indeed, having an impact on him. He allows Merton to sleep sometimes at the newly built, cinderblock hermitage. Merton writes, "I felt very much alive, real, awake, surrounded by silence and penetrated by truth."[30] By December 1964, Merton was able to stay a complete day at the hermitage, offering him a "sense of having arrived at last in the place destined for me by God, and for which I was brought here twenty-three years ago."[31]

By August 1965, Merton is living full-time at the hermitage. It is a transformative experience: "The five days I have had in real solitude have been a revelation. Whatever questions I may have had about it are answered. Over and over again I see that this life is what I have always hoped it would be and always sought. A life of peace, silence, purpose, meaning. It is not always easy but calls for a blessed and salutary effort. Everything about it is rewarding."[32]

He falls into a rhythm of manual labor in the morning and writing in the afternoon. He also has time to observe nature more closely, watching and delighting in the birds, squirrels, deer, the sky and the view offered by his large window. Merton is a happy man, and it is hard to imagine that this finally attained peace and serenity can be shattered, but Merton is soon to meet in a hospital a woman who would turn his life upside down.

# Chapter Nine

Whereas the three poems already discussed comment on individuation, depression, and the integration of the shadow, the poem "Hagia Sophia" addresses Merton's anima dilemma, what he refers to as "this great, stupid rift in my life, the refusal of woman."[1]

In 1958 Merton visits the home of his friend Victor Hammer in nearby Lexington, Kentucky. Hammer is a painter of spiritual themes as well as a publisher of rare, artistic editions of religious books. A traditionalist to the core, he has no use for the abstract expressionism art sweeping America (for example, Pollock, Rothko, de Kooning, Still, et al).

Delightedly viewing one painting after another, Merton comes to an abrupt halt before Hammer's unfinished triptych depicting a young woman's offering a crown to a young man. Merton becomes emotional. He questions Hammer about the identity of the woman (just as he had questioned his dream anima, Proverb). Hammer is unsure of the identity of the female figure, but the male figure is definitely Christ. Mystified, Merton keeps returning to the panel to peruse the features of the young maiden.

Why Merton's emotional response? It is not unlikely that Merton unconsciously recognized in the painting his own encounter with his dream anima. He is grappling with the whole concept of the feminine and her role in his life. Rather than attempting to identify the woman in the painting, Merton would be better served to decipher its symbolic meaning: The young woman (anima) offers a crown (a mandala symbol of wholeness) to a young man. Through the anima, wholeness is received, just as through Mary comes all grace. The young man represents every man who, when he accepts wholeness, takes upon himself Christ.

Not too long after his experience at the Hammers' home, on May 14, 1959, Merton writes to Mr. Hammer about "The feminine principle in the universe."[2]

This letter is the origin of the prose poem "Hagia Sophia." Let us look more closely at the structure of the poem and its message.

Merton arranges "Hagia Sophia" in the form of a quaternity, following the canonical hours of Lauds, Prime, Terce, and Compline. Jung considers quaternity as the symbol of wholeness. Since the poem concerns spiritual and psychic awareness, the poet devotes the first three sections of the poem to the new, morning light: during the hours of Lauds (5:30 a.m.), Prime (6:00 a.m.), and Terce (9:00 a.m.). The last section of the poem occurs after sunset, the hour of Compline, the time of the completion of the day's work and the monks' singing of the "Salve Regina."

In the first section, "Dawn, the Hour of Lauds," Merton, in the voice of the first-person singular (no persona is employed), compares himself to a man who has just awakened from sleep:

I am awakened, I am born again at the voice of this
my Sister, sent to me from the depths of the divine
fecundity.[3]

The Sister (from now on referred to as Anima) is Merton's anima, who "rises" from the depths of the unconscious, "the divine fecundity," the locus of the archetypes. Anima brings to Merton a "hidden wholeness" whose origin lies even deeper in the psyche, in the "unseen roots of all created being"—the collective unconscious. Note that Anima, like Proverb, is the initiator of the encounter between her and Merton: Merton is "awakened."

Later in this section, Merton compares himself to a man in a hospital, and Anima is likened to a nurse who has "the touch of all life, the touch of the spirit." As a nurse ministers to a sick body (as opposed to the nurse who struck him in "The Anatomy of Melancholy"), Anima bestows wholeness of spirit upon Merton.[4] Anima, however, does not always appear to Merton. There was a time when he fought against her, resisted her, refused her, especially during his youth when he exploited many young women. Merton warns the reader that Anima will only come to a man when he is "little" and "helpless" and "poor" and "without defense": He must be a humble man, a man stripped of all masks, a man who understands he is *not* self-sufficient. Then the poet declares, "This is what it means to recognize Hagia Sophia." Hagia Sophia is Anima. Anima is Holy Wisdom, inviting Merton and all men "with unutterable sweetness to be awake and to live."

In the second section, "Early Morning, the Hour of Prime," Merton praises his Anima:

O blessed, silent one, who speaks everywhere!

Although the anima speaks to every man, she can only be heard in silence. Man, however, refuses to be silent, to listen. In the first-person plural, Merton identifies with *all* men who fail to listen to their anima:

We do not hear the soft voice, the gentle voice, the merciful and feminine.

"We do not hear" is the sad refrain of this section. Time and time again Merton emphasizes the importance of listening. He warns us that if we do not listen to the anima, we are denied her fruits: "mercy," "yielding love," "nonresistance," "nonreprisal," and "simplicity." Yet there are some men who listen to their anima, perhaps only one man in a hundred thousand. The man, listening to his anima, "has come out of the confused primordial dark night into consciousness." He is the individuated man who survives the dark night of the soul because he "has expressed the clear silence of Sophia in his own heart." Merton also states that every man's individuation is of infinite importance, "the heavenly lights rejoice in the going forth of one man to make a new world in the morning."

In the next section, "High Morning, the Hour of Tierce," Merton evokes the spirit of the fourteenth century:

> (When the recluses of the fourteenth century England heard their Church bells and looked out upon the wolds and fens under a kind sky, they spoke in their hearts to "Jesus our Mother." It was Sophia that awakened in their childlike care.)

Merton clearly is referring to the fourteenth-century mystic Julian of Norwich, who lovingly invokes Jesus as our mother in her *Revelations of Divine Love*. Merton commences his poem in the first-person singular, then moves to the inclusive first-person plural, and he now joins his voice with the mystic of the fourteenth century who possessed the wisdom to recognize and accept the feminine in God. At one point in the poem, Merton boldly announces to the reader:

> All the perfections of created things are also in God;
> and therefore He is at once Father and Mother.

The motherhood of God was a daring concept in the fourteenth century, and it remains one in our time (cf. Benedict XVI, *Jesus of Nazareth* [New York: Doubleday, 2008]). For Merton, however, to be attracted to this feminine image of God indicates that he is, indeed, coming to terms with his own negative experience of motherhood, ("perhaps solitaries are made by severe mothers").[5] Merton's attraction to the loving, compassionate Lady Julian is a far cry from the monk who earlier in his spiritual life was enamored of the severe, ascetic mystic St. John of the Cross.

Lady Julian's message is *love*: God loves us "not with blame but with pity." To Julian God promised, "All manner of thing shall be well," a phrase used by Eliot in his "Four Quartets"). Merton says of Julian:

> Julian is without doubt one of the most wonderful of all Christian voices. She gets greater and greater in my eyes as I grow older and whereas in the old days I used to be crazy about St. John of the Cross, I would not exchange him now for Julian if you gave me the world and the Indies and all the Spanish mystics rolled up in one bundle.[6]

Much of the remainder of this section of the poem concerns Merton's attempt to *define* Sophia. He is always the man of intellect, employing her name more than ten times. He finally settles for an all-embracing definition of Hagia Sophia, of Anima, by recalling what he wrote to his friend Victor Hammer soon after he viewed Hammer's triptych:

> The feminine principle in the world is the inexhaustible source of creative realizations of the Father's glory. She is His manifestation in radiant splendor! But she remains unseen, glimpsed only by a few. Sometimes there are none who know her at all.

Merton has here amplified his original definition.

The last section, "Sunset, the Hour of Compline, Salve Regina" is the most hauntingly beautiful portion of the poem. We have arrived at the end of the monastic day when all Trappist monks assemble in the abbey church for the final singing of the psalms and the hymn, "Salve Regina." According to tradition, the church remains unlit, its darkness symbolizing the earth's approaching "sunset."

First, Merton meditates on the Virgin Mary, our mother, who is the "personal manifestation of Sophia." He then says that Mary is "perfect Creature" and "perfectly Redeemed" and "the perfect expression of wisdom in mercy." It is through Mary that "God enters into His creation." She is our Mother of mercy and our most gracious Advocate.

Merton then recalls his encounter with the mysterious young maiden of Victor Hammer's triptych:

> She crowns Him not with what is glorious, but with
> what is greater than glory, the one thing greater than
> glory is weakness, nothingness, poverty.

When he first viewed the triptych, he was perplexed about her identity. She was the *Unknown*. Merton has now moved *through* her mystery into an acceptance of her reality in his life and the life of the church. She is Sister, she is Anima, she is Hagia Sophia. She sent Christ "to die for us on the cross." She offers a crown of wholeness to every man because Christ accepted the crown of thorns, the Christ who still himself is "a homeless God, lost in the night, without papers, without identification." In the manner that Sophia is heard, so is he heard: in silence, in stillness, in darkness.

Later, Merton indeed falls in love with his nurse, mysteriously foretold in "Hagia Sophia." He named her M. Merton's journal entry for September 10, 1966, reads:

> I forgot to ask the exact date of her [M.'s] birthday but I think it is———.She was born just about two months before I came through Cincinnati on my way to Gethsemani! And I walked through Cincinnati station with the words of Proverb 8 in my mind: "And my delights were to be with the children of men!"—I have never forgotten this, it struck me so forcefully then! Strange connection in my deepest heart—between M. and the "Wisdom" figure—and Mary—and the Feminine in the Bible—Eve etc.—Paradise—wisdom. Most mysterious, haunting, deep, lovely, moving, transforming![7]

Jungian Maria von France writes:

> As Jung has demonstrated, the nucleus of the psyche (the self) normally expresses itself in some kind of fourfold structure. The number four is also connected with the anima because, as Jung noted, there are four stages in its development. The first stage is best symbolized by the figure of Eve, which represents purely instinctual and biological relations. The second can be seen in Faust's Helen: She personifies a romantic and aesthetic level that is, however, still characterized by sexual elements. The third is represented, for instance, by the Virgin Mary—a figure who raises love (*eros*) to the heights of spiritual devotion. The fourth type is symbolized by Sapientia, wisdom transcending even the most holy and the most pure.[8]

It is amazing how accurately Merton's journey correlates with Jung's theory of individuation, particularly his encounter with the anima archetype. There is another astonishing synchronicity: In the summer of 1986, Michael Mott discovered a drawing by Merton done in 1941, one he had never seen, called "Christ unveils the Meaning of the Old Testament." Mott describes the drawing:

> In the drawing Christ stands in the background unveiling the head and shoulders of a woman in the foreground. The woman, probably sitting, faces us but looks past us to her right. The face is fully revealed and drawn with great care. The woman has long, dark, free-falling hair. The eyes are large, beautiful, but underscored with line or shadow, as if to show grief, hunger, a certain fear or poverty, or, perhaps, all these.…The drawing is arresting in itself. In the life of Thomas Merton, it means that by 1941 he had decided upon the physical features of Proverb. These would reappear later for him in the Proverb/Sophia of 1959, after the dream of the Jewish girl he reports to Pasternak and after he has seen the painting by Victor Hammer.[9]

With "Hagia Sophia," Merton seems to have solved his anima problem, but his was an intellectual solution, one not based on experience of the feminine. For him truly to solve his "refusal of woman," he had to fall in love with a woman, and it is what actually happened. In "Hagia Sophia," he offers this description of himself (and the God within him):

> A vagrant, a destitute wanderer with dusty feet, finds his way down a new road…without even a number, a

frail expendable exile lies down in desolation under the
sweet stars of the world and entrusts Himself to sleep.

After years of self-examination, he knows himself all too
well: "I suppose I regret most my lack of love."[10]

Prior to entering the hospital in March 1966, Merton is
blissfully living in his hermitage. He has what he so longed for,
a place of his own where he could experience a deeper solitude,
a deeper silence. Merton has the silence, he has the solitude, and
he has the love of God and his community. But he has *not* experienced an overwhelming passion for another human being, neither with the woman with whom he fathered a child nor with the
many women he dated, like Ginny Burton. It perhaps never happened to Merton because he himself never felt he was lovable.
The other possible reason is his own doubt that he is capable of
passionately loving another person. All this soon changes when
he enters a Louisville hospital for an operation on his back in
mid-March 1966.

Before we address his falling in love, let us look at the kind
of life he is living in his hermitage before meeting his nurse M.
Merton has for years been reading Rainer Maria Rilke, a favorite
poet of Merton's, one he even shared with his novices, teaching
them how to read and "understand" him. There is a wonderful
tape, capturing his enthusiastic teaching of Rilke's poem "The
Panther," illustrating not only Merton's tremendous love of Rilke,
his knowledge and ability to read and speak German, but also
his great gift as a teacher of literature. He has an infectious love
for the written word and is a close reader, practicing well what
the French call *explication de texte*.

What enthralls Merton about Rilke is the poet's love of solitude and his ability to look at something so long and hard that
the poet seemingly disappears, becoming one with the observed.
In one of his poems, Rilke exclaims, "You must change your life."

Merton takes up this challenge in the hermitage. He becomes acutely aware of everything:

> The morning got more and more brilliant and I could feel the brilliancy of it getting into my own blood. Living so close to the cold, you feel the spring. And this is man's mission! The earth cannot feel all this. We must. But living away from the earth and the trees we fail them. We are absent from the wedding feast.[11]

His is a Rilkean existence. Merton is exquisitely alive, but what is missing are human beings. It was Rilke's major deprivation: people. Merton once observed that Rilke was a bit narcissistic, but he admired him because he felt that Rilke *allowed* solitude to find him. This says much about Merton's obsession with solitude, for he seems to be the *opposite* of Rilke; he set out to possess solitude, finally "winning" his own hermitage.

His life becomes one of exquisite attention. When he walks in the woods, he feels it is far more important than "a lot of analysis and a lot of reporting on the things 'of the spirit.'"[12] He finds himself watching the patterns of water in a local creek. He spends time gazing at deer through field glasses and is entranced by their perfection.

In a moment of happiness, he confesses that his life in the hermitage is saner and better balanced than it was in the monastery. He looks forward to the future and is anxious to have his back operation over with so that he can "start afresh."[13]

He has had his operation and is now back at his hermitage. His April 19 journal entry is his first about M.: "And a letter from M. I was glad to hear from her. Have to think—my way around the problem of this tenderness—but anyway, I will do the only thing possible, and risk loving with Christ's love when there is no obvious need for it. And not fear!"[14]

Notice the use of the word *problem*. We have seen this term before. Also notice his willingness to take a risk. As a Trappist, he is a model monk. Yes, his fame makes it difficult for him to conform to the Rule of St. Benedict, but for the most part he *is* able to juggle being a monk *and* a writer. It is not easy, and he is often depressed by the pressures put on him by his superiors and by his fame, but he somehow manages to get through his muddles. Now he is to experience something that transfigures him and his life: falling in love. If his meeting Gregory Zilboorg was one of the most debilitating events of his life, his falling in love with M. is one of the most exhilarating and life-enhancing events. To deny himself the experience of loving M. would be tantamount to a kind of masochism, a wounding from which he would never recover.

Falling head over heels in love with M. is likely the best thing that could have happened to Merton. Jolande Jacobi writes:

> The encounter with anima…makes it possible for us to apprise ourselves of our contra-sexual traits in all their manifestations and to accept at least a part of the qualities projected on the partner as belonging to our own selves, though as a rule this is not accomplished without violent resistances. What man will recognize or accept his moodiness, his unreliability, his sentimentality, and all the other allegedly "feminine" vices, as his own characteristics instead of chalking them up to the nearest female in his vicinity? Once they are made conscious and are no longer projected, but are experienced as belonging to oneself, as realities and agencies within the psyche, anima and animus become symbols of its power to procreate and to give birth: everything new and creative owes its existence to them.[15]

Merton's falling in love with M. is a way to greater self-knowledge. During his time with M., he writes some of his best poetry, and his journal blazes with a liveliness and transparency that none of the other journals possess. In short, under M.'s influence, Merton becomes a *whole* man, capable of loving *and* being loved.

There is a cost, however, to pay for this wholeness. His "affair" with M. is a roller-coaster ride of emotions that ranges from serenity to joy to exhilaration, if not ecstasy, to feelings of worthlessness, anguish, guilt, and depression. As for M., we have only Merton's side of the love affair, though there are journal entries where Merton quotes M. verbatim.

The most fruitful way to attempt to understand what Merton experiences when he falls in love with M. is to read *Learning to Love*, volume 6 of his published journals. It is an aptly named journal: Loving a woman is a new heaven and earth for Merton, and he is confused and disturbed by it as well as absurdly happy. The cerebral man, who has led a highly intellectual life, is now at the mercy of his emotions, and he does not know how to cope with them. He is like a blind man walking in the dark, bumping into things he had no idea were there. At the same time, each "accident" is exhilarating, reminding him that there is so much of life of which he is unaware. M.'s love pulls Merton into the dance of life.

If we look at Merton's affair with M. as if it were a musical score, we see that its movement corresponds to a crescendo and a decrescendo with a silent, barely audible, resigned coda.

Let us ponder a few of Merton's journal entries:

Yesterday, the whole day revolved around a long (illegal) phone conversation with M. I got in the cellarer's office when everyone was at dinner…reached her in the hospital cafeteria (cry of joy when she found out who it was!)....Still we both know there is no future to it and there is no sense making much of it.[16]

❧

I have got to dare to love, and to bear the anxiety of self-questioning that love arouses in me.[17]

❧

...I have let love take hold of me in spite of all my fear and I have obeyed love.[18]

❧

Yet she is right to be scared. We can simply wreck each other.[19]

❧

I see how badly I need her love to complete me with its warmth and understanding.[20]

❧

I just don't know what to do with my life, finding myself too much loved, and loving so much, when according to all standards it is all wrong, absurd, insane.[21]

❧

At times I am so carried away by M. that I can't think of anything but of finding some way to spend the rest of my life with her.[22]

❧

I have surrendered again to a kind of inimical wom-
anly wisdom in M. which instinctively seeks out the
wound in me that most needs her sweetness, and lav-
ishes all her love upon me there....I feel less sick. I
feel human.[23]

Merton's candid revelations of love are so human and moving. He has never before been so transparent in his journals,
never before so unmasked and heartbreakingly vulnerable. He
gives his all to his journal, holding nothing back. He seems to
say, "See me as I am. If you thought I was a saint, you were
wrong. I am a flawed human being, *just like you*. And now this
astounding thing has happened to me, one I never expected: I
am in love with a beautiful woman, and if you can believe this,
she loves me too!"

There is, of course, a "problem" here: he is a *celibate* monk,
and by calling her and later meeting her, he is breaking all the
order's rules. Merton, in the midst of his affair with M., is reading Albert Camus, the great Nobel Prize-winning novelist who
wrote so eloquently about the modern world and absurdity.
Merton now finds himself in an absurd situation: a monk in love
with a woman.

Confronted, Merton has no answers. For many years, he has
served as a spiritual master par excellence for millions of readers,
advising them how to live a good, holy Christian life, how to foster a closer relationship with God, how to love God. He is now a
man confused; now the only certain thing in his life is that he
loves M. How does he *feel* (not what he *thinks*, because his life
thus far has been imbalanced by intellectual dominance) about
being in love? In his own words, he feels "human." He further
states, "I am glad of my love for M., which adds a special note of

absurdity and therefore of reality to my professed 'solitude.' It is in many ways the best thing that could have happened."[24]

The affair, however, imposes a great pressure on Merton. He confesses to being sexually aroused, so much so that he fears a "crack-up."[25] As a priest and as a monk who has taken vows, he understands his affair is objectively wrong, but paradoxically it is *right* for him. To use Camus' expression, it is "absurd" because it is not rational, not reasonable; in short, it makes no sense—except that in his life *now*, it makes eminent good sense: He *needs* to love and to be loved. For once in his adult life, he decides to obey *not* institutional life but the instinctual life.

Merton turns Camus' approach to absurdity on its head, particularly Camus' conclusion that one must face life's absurdity with bravery. Merton contradicts him, declaring that the life of Sisyphus is not particularly tragic or futile. It is not futile, he says, if you simply live it. Thus, Merton can say with conviction, "What does the lonely and absurd man have to teach others? Simply that being alone and absurd are not things to be feared."[26]

By loving M., Merton has confronted an "absurd" problem. If you need a key to solve the problem, then there is only one thing to do: Emulate Sisyphus and do what you *have* to do. Merton loves M., and he will have to face the consequences of his loving M., which include being discovered by Abbot Fox and being ordered to end the affair.

For a long time, Merton has been recording his dreams. Let us look at two dreams that shed light on Merton's love for M.

> June 25, 1966
>
> Dream—"another" girl. I am supposed to date her soon but now she is in the hospital. I am talking to her mother (a heavy mother—battle-axe type), not interested in any of them much. But then someone suggests we go and see this girl in the hospital and I

feel an inner awakening of interest and love, and I
know that briefly seeing her will awaken in us both a
deeper rapport. I then wake up thinking—but this is
another; not M., and go back to thinking consciously
of M. with a little guilt. Is it another? Imagery later—
after difficulty starting—

I see a tangle of dark briars and light roses. My
attention singles out one beautiful pink rose, which
becomes luminous, and I am much aware of the silky
texture of the petals. My Mother's face appears behind
the roses, which vanish!

Also in here somewhere a student nurse who came
to see me briefly in hospital one day when I was
preparing to go out for a walk. I was short and rude
with her.[27]

Many of Merton's dreams occur in hospitals, suggesting a
need for healing. There is an unflattering woman ("battle-axe
type") and a girl who is *not* M. The anima is multifaced, confus-
ing Merton, ever a cerebral man needing to articulate his thoughts
and ideas.

In the dream, he moves from actual women to symbols of
a woman: The woman is a luminous pink rose but discerned
through a tangle of dark briars. It reflects Merton's current situation: He must view his pink rose (M.) through the many obstacles (briars like spying monks, Abbot Fox, secret phone calls and
clandestine meetings) that he has to somehow overcome either
by stealth or by overtly breaking monastic rules.

His mother's face then appears out of nowhere, and the
roses vanish. Not a good omen: Mother was stinting in her
expression of love and her son described her as "severe" and
"cerebral." She, therefore, represents a threat to his positive relationship with M.

His student nurse visits him in the monastery. She obviously represents M., and he is brusque and rude. Is it because of the appearance of a negative anima (Mother) image, causing him to feel bad about himself, to feel unworthy of M? There is seemingly no permanent damage done. On awakening, he remembers that this is the day he will gift M. with his *Midsummer Diary* (part of volume 6 of his journals), especially written for her.

The *Midsummer Diary* contains some of Merton's most beautiful writing and profound thought. Its transparency, its anguish, its longing, and its vulnerable humanity leave one breathless.

Even though Merton admits to loving M. in the depths of his heart, he knows in his heart that his love for M. will not follow a normal course: a long, warm, slow-growing, sweet love; it will be "amputated just when it was about to begin."[28] To make matters worse, there is nothing either of them can do about it. Merton concludes that the outcome is "cruel."[29]

At times, Merton feels that he has made a "mess of everything." The only consolation: "You cannot love without getting hurt."[30] Merton who had once espoused a *contemptus mundi* is now very much a part of the human family, not a safely sequestered monk in a hermitage. He is, however, realistic, admitting that marriage is out of the question: "It would destroy me."[31]Again, there is another consolation: "There is no going back to the time when I did not love her."[32] It is the kind of consolation reminiscent of Tennyson's, " 'Tis better to have loved and lost / Than never to have loved at all" ("In Memoriam," 1850).

At the end of the *Midsummer Diary*, Merton, as a writer, is at his most eloquent, his prose so moving that one must turn to diarists like Samuel Pepys, Julian Green, or Virginia Woolf to find its equivalent. Merton writes:

> Why do I live alone? I don't know. The whole question of my love for M. has got me backed up to the

wall on this particular choice. As if there were a choice. Actually there is not even a choice, really. I have to lead this absurd existence. In some mysterious way I am condemned to it. Not as to something wonderful and mysterious, but as though to a vice. I cannot have enough of the hours of silence when nothing happens. When the clouds go by. When the trees say nothing. When the birds sing. I am completely addicted to the realization that just being there is enough, and to add something else is to mess it all up....I am flawed. I am nuts. I can't help it. Here I am, now sweated up, in a misty foul summer evening when all is loused up to my neck, happy as a coot. The whole business of saying I am flawed is a lie. I am happy. I cannot explain it. I cannot justify it by pretending I am guilty. I love you darling, I love you in this mad life that I lead. I miss you. I wish I could see you, I wish I could hold you and love you, but I cannot be tied to any living being. I just cannot be tied.[33]

It is important to note that at the end of his affair with M., Merton, on September 8, 1967, signed (as did Abbot Fox) a short formula he himself drafted (although he was very likely under pressure to do so). It reads:

Thursday the 8th I made my commitment—read the short formula I had written (simplest possible form). Dom James signed it with me, content that he now had me in the bag as an asset that would not go out and lose itself in some crap game (is he sure—? The crap game of love). A commitment "to live in solitude for the rest of my life in so far as health may permit."[34]

The word *asset* is particularly revelatory. He was, indeed, a valuable asset to Gethsemani, having brought much needed capital into a monastery once on the verge of financial ruin. When Merton became a monk, he took a vow of poverty; thus, he had no access to "his" money. It is also interesting to note here that although Michael Mott studiously avoids in his biography of Merton the word *depression*, he finally admits that Merton, indeed, suffered from it. Writing about Merton's journals, Mott says:

> If they (journals) preserved the spontaneity, they preserved the scandal, the whole man (whole, sometimes, to the point of exhaustion). The pages on God, on prayer, on humility, would distress some; the pages of criticism of the Church would worry many; the praise of the Church, others; references to drinking, to dreams, to periods of depression—references to his own evasions, to his capacity for kidding himself, to his less than an honest lover, to costly mistakes of fact and judgment....When he was used, or used up, the journals would speak of him without editing, crossing-out, polishing—a place where the narrow-minded, or those who had made a cult of him, would founder, and where the seekers of truth would find him.[35]

We are indeed fortunate to have his journals: Merton made sure we would be able to see him without his repertoire of masks, to see him as he really was.

On September 21, 1966, Merton records the following dream:

> A dream. I know that M. is swimming alone in one of our lakes. I am near there but I have refrained from joining her for fear of the consequences. But now I approach the lake and see her wading in the water over

there by the shore (it is no recognizable lake here—
what is it like?) She looks so disconsolate and alone, as
if she had wasted her afternoon there to no purpose,
since I have not come. I go down toward the lake
dressed in my habit and wave to her that I am coming.
She still looks disconsolate, unbelieving. I wish to join
her, I think, even if I have to swim naked. There appears
to be no one around. But as I go to her along the bank
I find one of the monks sitting there in my way. I cannot get to her. At this I wake up in great distress.[36]

(Note that this dream occurred eleven days after he wrote
and signed his agreement to Abbot Fox not to leave Gethsemani.)[37]

Merton longs to join M. in the water. He is bothered that
she looks so sad and alone. As he approaches the bank, he is
intent on joining her even if he has to remove his habit and swim
naked. He then notices one of the monks (a shadow figure), and
he decides he *cannot* go to her. He is afraid of the consequences
of joining her. He also fears his own desires as well as disobey-
ing his abbot, who ordered him not to see her again.

Notice that the anima figure is described as disconsolate
and alone; it is likely how M. feels in real life after the breakup.
But Merton wears a habit, symbolizing his vocation as a monk
and a priest. He is not at liberty to join M. either in his dream or
real life.

The dream serves as a warning to Merton: He must renounce
M. or face the consequences, which could be severe.

Let us now look at two more dreams, which shed more
light on his life:

Last night—curious dreams. One—I am in a place
where there are Buddhist nuns, separated from me by
a curious, paper-thin sort of iconostasis or printed

> partition, behind which I hear their soft erotic laugh-
> ter as they are aware of me there. Sense of being
> drawn to them.[38]

We are again reminded of Merton's "refusal of woman." As
mentioned before, there were many women in Merton's life, his
mother, grandmother, his Aunt Maud, his father's lovers, including the novelist Evelyn Scott, who was particularly cruel to
Merton, the girl with whom he fathered a child, and the many
women he dated, Sylvia, Joan and Ginny Burton at the top of the
list along with Andrew Winser's sister, the young girl he never, of
course, dated but whom he never forgot.

He seemingly always had women in his life, so some may
wonder what he truly meant by his "refusal of woman." This dream
helps us understand his dilemma. The women are Buddhist nuns,
indicative of his interest in the East; but women, regardless of philosophy or religion, attract Merton although there always seems to
be something to prevent a connection with them. In this dream, it
is a "paper-thin iconostasis." The separation could easily be broken
through, but it is like an iconostasis, a holy wall often decorated
with the images of Mary, Christ, or the saints. He hears their "erotic
laughter" beyond and is drawn to them. In a normal situation, a
man would break through and go to them. But the dream reflects
his life. Merton wears an "iconostasis"; it is his Cistercian habit: He
is an ordained priest and a professed monk; "paper-thin," it *can* easily be removed, but he dons the iconostasis himself. Yes, he can
"break" through it any time he wants, and he has done so with M.,
but he agreed to sign an agreement with Abbot Fox, choosing to
remain at Gethsemani and not leave with M.

Here is the other dream:

> The monastery building (Gethsemani) is on fire. The
> fire burns slowly on the inside of the building, but

threatens to become violent. Meanwhile, there are still people in the building. I think "Why don't they get out?" I myself am there, moving through small patches of fire, but get to safety. The building is not destroyed but all that is inside is consumed, more or less.[39]

There are several ways to interpret Merton's dream. The burning abbey could be Merton himself consumed by erotic passion. The fire is "violent," and he wonders why the people (shadow aspects of himself) in the building just don't get out. Interpretation: *Why doesn't he leave Gethsemani before he is destroyed by his own erotic passions?*

Or we could interpret the dream as one of purgation. Merton remains at Gethsemani because the fire of its discipline will help him find his True Self. Notice that although the *contents* of the abbey are consumed by fire, the *building* remains standing. We could say the same of Merton: He has had an eventful life at Gethsemani, passionate about a number of things: ideas, books, solitude, silence, hermit life, Vatican II (1962–65), theology, and a passionate affair with M. He is a man fully alive, of enormous energy, gifted with a Picasso-like gusto for life. He has, however, remained at Gethsemani because he knows deep in his heart that it is the only place where he will purge (burn) himself of the false selves that keep him from his True Self.

The affair is over by September of 1966 (M. visits him one more time when he is in the hospital in October). In December, he is visited by the folk singer Joan Baez. During his romance with M., it is Baez's "Silver Dagger" that Merton finds himself singing to himself, a song about the risks and dangers of love. Perhaps the song meant so much to Merton because of the last line: in the end, the narrator is resigned to spending the rest of life sleeping alone. He knows in his heart it is to be his destiny. Joan Baez, however, is sympathetic to his plight. Moved by his narration of his love affair with M., she offers to drive him to Cincinnati so that he could see M. But in his mind and heart, he has ended the affair.

He did, however, receive a Christmas card from M. Merton writes:

> A card from M. today: thought of her suddenly the other day, almost saw her it was so vivid. That was the day the card was mailed. From C——, not M——. Certainly I feel less real, somehow, without our constant communication, our sense of being in communion (so intense last year). The drab, futile silences of this artificial life, with all its tensions and its pretenses: but I know it would be worse somewhere else. And marriage, for me would be terrible! Anyway, that's all over. In a month I'll be 53, and no one in his right mind would get married for the first time at such an age.
>
> Yet this afternoon I wondered if I'd really missed the point of life after all. A dreadful thought![40]

The year 1967 is a calmer one for Merton although he is a permanently changed man, in his own eyes and in the eyes of his abbot. He explains to theologian Rosemary Ruether (known for her antimonasticism) that he is considered a "maverick in the Order." He informs her that his abbot believes he is ready to run off with a woman any day; thus, he is under constant surveillance. Having a hermitage, he further explains, is just an attempt by the abbot to keep him "under wraps."[41]

He commits a faux pas by referring to Ruether as a "cerebral" woman, and she takes umbrage. Merton mollifies her by saying that his mother was cerebral, explaining, "'Cerebral' probably because I resented my mother's intellectuality (or what I later interpreted as that)."[42] Even in 1967, he remembers his mother vividly, and he likely remembers that when his brother was born, he was no longer the center of his mother's attention, a possible cause of his resentment against his brother and subsequent lifelong guilt about not treating his brother kindly when they were children. In another letter to Ruether, he says, "I am not mad at you for being an 'intellectual woman' but only for seeming to reject me. I don't take to rejection, I tell you."[43] A telling remark, indeed.

During his correspondence with Ruether, he records in his journal a candid summary of his life:

> What is "wrong" in my life is not so much a matter of "sin" (though it is sin too), but of unawareness, lostness, slackness, relaxation, dissipation of desire, lack of courage and of decision, so that I let myself be carried along and dictated to by an alien movement. The current of "the world," which I know is not mine. I am always getting diverted to a way that is not my way and is not going where I am called to go. And only if I go where I must go can I be of any use to "the world." I can serve the world best keeping my distance and my freedom.[44]

Some would argue that he has in most cases "diverted" himself, and that he had had more choices in his life than his fellow brothers at Gethsemani.

The question to ask at this point is: Did Merton's love affair with M. help make him a better man or was it a temptation he was well rid of? The (or at least my) answer is: He was profoundly changed for the better. Even though he burned his love letters, they were surely forever inscribed in his heart.

Jane Polden writes:

> Love itself is a basic force in nature, a developmental force leading towards connection and growth. Through

our willingness to reach out imaginatively towards others, we transcend ourselves and become one with this force. As we do so, the context within which we live our own lives expands. Love has been described as the willingness to extend oneself in the service of one's own or another's spiritual growth: the act of loving is an act of self-transcendence—a choice, not an emotion, a leap outside the prison of conformity and the narrow boundaries of the ego into the unknown, a process of spiritual evolution which is capable of growing from strength to strength.[45]

Spiritual growth surely occurs, with Merton and with M., and if we have to describe Merton in the very last years of his life, before he set off for the East, what can we say? Monica Furlong offers this final portrait of the monk Thomas Merton:

What Merton found in the desert, in place of his old world hating self, was a passionate love of the world, an intense enjoyment of nature, a deep love for other human beings, women as well as men, and a wonderful gaiety and humor.[46]

His journals reveal, however, that M. is constantly on his mind, and he still dreams of her. The coda to the whole affair, however, is found in an entry recorded on August 20, 1968. Merton writes:

Today, among other things, I burned M.'s letters. Incredible stupidity in 1966! I did not glance at any one of them. High hot flames of the pine branches in the sun.[47]

Some people are astonished (even disturbed) that Merton burned M.'s letters. Merton, however, has again donned his Catholic author mask. He is also preparing for his trip to the East. He has burned other papers too, likely sensitive, revelatory ones. M. had lost Merton's letters to her in a move, so by destroying her letters, he leaves behind no record of the affair except his own, in the form of poetry and journal. It may have been his way of protecting M. from future scrutiny. As for describing his affair as an "incredible stupidity"—well, he had said that what they were involved in was absurd, but to interpret his remark as dismissive of M. or his love for her and her love for him would indeed be absurd and unfair—to both the monk and the nurse.

# Chapter Ten

By the 1960s Merton is fully aware that there is in the world a thing called "Mertonism." He dislikes it and complains to friends about it, but for better or worse, he has a following that watches his every move and reads his every new book.

He begins to take seriously the move to preserve his papers in the Merton Collection at Bellarmine College. He is glad to hear that Frank Dell'Isola is putting together an official bibliography. He begins to keep copies of his letters. It is unfortunate that he not was as scrupulous in the 1940s or we would have access to his missing "Novitiate Journal."

Merton is, however, ambivalent about the Merton Collection:

> Ambiguities at work here: the pretended "roots" at Gethsemani, where I am alien and where most everyone else is alien too....Merton Room again—ambiguity of an open door that is closed. Of a cell where I don't really live. Where my papers live. Where my papers are more than I am. I myself am open and closed. Where I reveal most I hide most. There is still something I have not said; but what it is I don't know, and maybe I have to say it by not saying.[1]

He seemingly mocks the existence of a room to contain his archives, but during his life he paradoxically makes a point of saving his papers before he enters Gethsemani: He leaves his poems in the safe keeping of Mark Van Doren; he saves his novels and sends papers to Sister Therese Lentfoehr; he mails a carbon copy of his autobiography to Boston College, where it is still archived. Perhaps the "closed" part of himself—about which he cannot freely write—is a reference to the fact that he never writes about his son, an ever-present wound, and as Harold Talbott remarked, the key to his life.

His ambivalent comments about the Merton Room make one question how much Merton truly reveals in his writings. How maskless, for instance, are his journals? He rarely writes about his prayer life except in theoretical terms. He rarely comments upon how he prays, and he never indicates whether or not he has ever experienced unitive prayer, the goal of most contemplatives.

He writes about Jesus, but he rarely comments on his personal relationship with Jesus. The reason may be a simple one, related to what William James describes as the "ineffable." By this, James means that when one has to write about the spiritual, particularly about the mystical, one discovers that words are inadequate to express the inexpressible. Because words are all we have, however, we are reduced to trying to describe prayer and the presence of God in our lives—yet our efforts are too often fraught with clichés.

There is also the matter of Merton's privacy: He believed that there are parts of one's soul that no one but God should have access to; it is what Merton (borrowing from Massignon) refers to as the *temps vièrge*, the virgin point within: a place where one is alone with the Alone—and to write about it would cheapen his spirituality.

On September 7, 1967, Dom James Fox announces his plan to resign as abbot of Gethsemani. Ironically, Dom Fox now wishes to be a hermit, having already chosen the place of his hermitage to be located on the Edelen Farm property (the spot Merton first chose for himself), far more secluded than Merton's hermitage.

Dom Flavian Burns is elected abbot of Gethsemani on January 13, 1968. Merton is delighted. He will definitely have more freedom under Burns's leadership.

Before Burns's election, Merton writes about his vocation as not one that includes public speaking, but that it may be right and necessary, at times, to speak to small groups in monastic-like settings. Soon after, he records his receiving an invitation from Dom Jean Leclerq to attend a monastic-ecumenical meeting in Bangkok. The new sympathetic abbot, Flavian Burns, would make the decision.

Burns takes his time about making his decision, but he allows Merton other visits: to California and New Mexico. Merton enjoys staying with the Trappistine nuns of Our Lady of the Redwoods, and he also travels to New Mexico to visit Christ in the Desert Monastery, a place that greatly impresses him; yet he finds himself homesick for Gethsemani. He writes, "A journey is a bad death if you ingeniously grasp or remove all that you were before you started, so that in the end you do not change in the least. The stimulation enables you to grasp more raffishly at the same familiar, distorted illusions. You come home only confirmed in greater greed—with new skills (real or imaginary) for satisfying it. I am not going home. The purpose of this death is to become homeless."[2]

Back at his hermitage, he is happy to see his chapel's icons, Ad Reinhardt's small painting of a cross, the Shaker Tree of Life in the kitchen, and the calligraphic scroll from Suzuki hanging on the wall. This is his home, and it now has an added luxury: a modern bathroom. He possesses everything he dreamed of: He has his hermitage, and now the added boon of travel. Later, Abbot Burns approves his trip to Bangkok.

It is natural to wonder how different it was for Merton to live under the rule of Dom Flavian Burns. Merton writes:

What a difference between Fr. Flavian, as abbot, and
Dom James. And what a difference in our relationship. I get a real sense of openness, of possibilities, of
going somewhere—and at times it is almost incredible. I seem to be dreaming.[3]

Abbot Burns is open to the idea of Merton's starting a small
hermit colony on the West Coast near the Redwoods convent,
places Merton has already visited, like Bear Harbor, Needle
Rock, and Ettersburg. There is also the possibility of starting
something in New Mexico; in fact, Merton is overwhelmed by
the "possibilities."

He eagerly plots his trip to Bangkok with stops at Calcutta
and Darjeeling before reaching Bangkok. After visits to several
monasteries in the states, he flies from San Francisco to
Honolulu. From there he flies to Japan and finally arrives in
Bangkok on October 17, 1968.

Merton meets Harold Talbott in New Delhi. He forgets that
he had already met him. As a Harvard student, Talbott was confirmed at Gethsemani, having received a blessing from Merton.
Talbott is now a student of the Dalai Lama, and he has arranged
a meeting between the two spiritual leaders, one that Merton is
excited about, hoping for an opportunity not only to discuss the
Tibetan religion but also to visit a Tibetan monastery.

The first meeting with the Dalai Lama occurs on November
4, 1968. They discuss Tibetan mysticism, and the Dalai Lama
advises Merton to develop a foundation in Madhyamika philosophy as well as consult a fine, well-versed Tibetan scholar who
has learned to unite both study and practice. They also discuss
*dzogchen*, defined as "the simplest and most beneficial way to
rediscover instantly for oneself the transcendental awareness that
is within, whose all-inclusive qualities are either presently active
or lying latent in human beings."[4]

Merton also jots down in his journal a reflection about the "wounded metaphysician," clearly a reference to himself:

> The metaphysician as wounded man. A wounded man is not an agnostic—he just has different questions, arising out of his wound. Recognition of the wound as a substitute for real identity, when one can "think of nothing else."[5]

This entry echoes Wallace Stevens's concept of the modern poet as a "metaphysician in the dark." Merton remains a wounded man, and he admits that all his questions arise from his own unique woundedness, but he also understands that one cannot identify with one's woundedness and build an identity around it. The use of wounds, he implies, is that it spurs us on to understand ourselves and to seek the source of the wound and its cure.

After his first meeting with the Dalai Lama, Merton reflects about his life and future. He is beginning to be more appreciative of his hermitage at Gethsemani because even in the mountains at the Dalai Lama's retreat, he finds that crowds and noise cannot be avoided. Real solitude is very difficult to achieve no matter where he goes although he feels that Alaska is perhaps the best place for him. There are other places, however, that he also wants to check out: Scotland, Switzerland, and Wales.

After this meeting, Merton has the following dream:

> Last night I dreamed that I was, temporarily, back at Gethsemani. I was dressed in a Buddhist monk's habit, but with more black and red and gold, a "Zen habit," in color more Tibetan than Zen. I was going to tell Brother Donald (Kane), the cook, in the diet kitchen, that I would be there for supper. I met some

women in the corridor, visitors and students of Asian religion, to whom I was explaining I was a kind of Zen monk and Gelugpa (Tibetan monk) together, when I woke up.[6]

His dream reveals his high respect for Tibetan religion. It also underscores his desire to understand it, to become it, to be dressed in its habit even when he is back at Gethsemani (wearing an Eastern habit could also be considered a subversive act, Merton ever a rebel). He has previously written about his desire to unite the Eastern and Western church within himself, thus establishing unification; this dream reveals a similar desire: he wants to nullify Kipling's idea that "East is East and West is West / And never the twain shall meet."

Merton, however, believes that they can indeed meet, in each individual's willingness to "dress" in the "black, and red and gold." Wearing a Zen habit or a Tibetan habit is symbolic of acceptance and assimilation; it is also a sign of approval. His meeting with the abbey's cook is an allusion to nourishment, food for the body, but there is also needed nourishment for the soul; thus, Eastern religions have much to teach and to nourish us.

The appearance of women in his dream as well as "students of religion" (he is a perennial student of religion) reveals that Merton feels more comfortable with women, now present in a cloistered monastery (a mirror of his once cloistered mind where the anima was absent or, rather, ignored). It also suggests that everyone at Gethsemani is a student of religion, that monks are forever learning about God, the great unknowable. In short, his dream underscores the profound effect the Dalai Lama has exerted on him.

In his own way, Merton has for a long time been a subversive monk at Gethsemani. Ignoring disapproval, he has opened himself to other religions by studying Zen Buddhism and the

Sufis, as well as Tibetan texts. With Vatican II's influence, he can now do so in the open, without secrecy and without reprimand.

During the second meeting, Merton and the Dalai Lama discuss epistemology and *samadhi*. Merton states that it is important for monks to be living examples of freedom and transformation, the fruit of the practice of meditation. The Dalai Lama agrees that meditation is indeed important, and he also stresses the vital importance of posture in Tibetan meditation as well as concentration on the mind. The Dalai Lama demonstrates the sitting position that is essential for meditation as well as explaining the meaning of *samadhi*.

The last meeting with the Dalai Lama Merton considers the best. Merton writes:

> My third interview with the Dalai Lama was in some ways the best. He asked a lot of questions about Western monastic life, particularly the vows, the rule of silence, the ascetic way, etc. But what concerned him most was:
>
> 1. Did the "vows" have any connection with a spiritual transmission or initiation?
> 2. Having made vows, did the monks continue to progress along a spiritual way, toward an eventual illumination, and what were the degrees of that progress? And supposing a monk died without having attained to perfect illumination? What ascetic methods were used to help purify the mind of passions? He is interested in the "mystical life," rather than in external observance.[7]

At this final meeting, Merton finally broaches politics because he is interested in the Dalai Lama's reaction to his notes on the theme he is to address at Bangkok: "Marxism and Monasticism." The Dalai Lama is frank and insightful, commenting that if Marxism concerned itself only with economic equality, it would perhaps not be dangerous. It becomes dangerous when it interferes with or suppresses religion. The Dalai Lama also stresses the importance of detachment, a virtue also praised by Christianity, for the detached man or woman is free of danger.

At the end of the meeting, the Dalai Lama calls Merton a Catholic *geshe*. Harold Talbott explains to Merton that he had received the highest compliment from the Dalai Lama: It was "like an honorary doctorate!"[8]

His last journal contains his reflections about whether or not he will stay at Gethsemani. He writes that he should not permanently separate himself from Gethsemani and that he should also spend his last days there. Before the end, however, he prefers to live as a hermit either in Alaska or around the Redwoods area. He requires greater silence and solitude, certain he will have neither at Gethsemani.

We now come to Merton's visiting the Polonnaruwa Buddhas. Much has been written about his experience of gazing upon the Buddhas when he is "suddenly, almost forcibly, jerked clean out of the habitual, half-tired vision of things, and an inner clearness, clarity, as if exploding from the rocks themselves, became evident and obvious."[9]

Let it be noted, his experience cannot be nailed down. Merton himself could not fully capture it in words: His is an ineffable experience, one of the most if not *the* most profound of his life. In Jungian terms, Merton's experience points toward his final integration. Strangely enough, Merton writes an essay named "Final Integration" in which he states:

> Final integration is a state of transcultural maturity far beyond mere social adjustment, which always implies

partiality and compromise. The man who is "fully born" has an entirely "inner experience of life." He apprehends his life fully and wholly from an inner ground that is at once more universal than the empirical ego and yet entirely his own. He is in a certain sense "cosmic" and "universal man." He has attained a deeper, fuller identity than that of his limited ego-self which is only a fragment of his being. He is in a certain sense identified with everybody: or in the familiar language of the New Testament…he is "all things to men."[10]

Without doubt, Merton became the person he wrote about: he is integrated, whole, cosmic, and universal. When he steps barefoot upon the wet grass before the Polonnaruwa Buddhas, he steps upon holy ground. He also steps upon the ground of being. He is more himself, more grounded than he has ever been in his life: In an instant he is "jerked clean out of himself"; thus, in the familiar language of the New Testament, he experiences Christ's promise that "in losing yourself you will find yourself."

Merton's description of his experience before the Polonnaruwa Buddhas is extraordinary writing:

Looking at these figures I was suddenly, almost forcibly, jerked clean out of the habitual, half-tired vision of things, and an inner clearness, clarity, as if exploding from the rocks themselves, became evident and obvious. The sheer evidence of the reclining figure, the smile the sad smile of Ananda standing with arms folded (much more "imperative" than Da Vinci's Mona Lisa because completely simple and straightforward). The thing about all this is that there is no puzzle, nor problem and really no "mystery."…I mean, I know and have seen what I was obscurely looking for. I don't know what else remains but I have seen and have pierced through the surface and have got beyond the shadow and the disguise.[11]

Notice Merton's leap from gazing at the Buddha's smile to commenting on the smile of the Mona Lisa. Merton's attention is drawn to the Buddha's smile because it is "imperative": It is commanding in a more simple way than the smile of the Mona Lisa, which is an enigmatic smile, far from straightforward; thus, its perennial fascination for countless viewers.

We do not, however, have to deconstruct Merton's reaction to the Buddhas: He is drawn to its whole beauty, its shape, line, and design, and especially its smile. We think of Simone Weil's definition of beauty: "The beauty of the world is Christ's tender smile for us coming through matter. He is really present in the universal beauty. The love of this beauty proceeds from God dwelling in our souls and goes out to God present in the universe. It also is like a sacrament."[12]

In a timeless moment, the Christ in Merton reaches out to the Christ in the beauty of the Polonnaruwa Buddhas.

Then there is Merton's startling comment, "I have now seen and pierced through the surface and have got beyond the shadow and the disguise." To see beyond the shadow is to see its opposite: the light. A Zen Buddhist might say that Merton became an enlightened man. To pierce the disguise is to see beyond all masks, all personae, to see the True Self; therefore, he experiences a glimpse of God, for our True Self is Christ: "Not I but Christ in me." A Christian may indeed say that Merton has had an authentic mystical experience.

In the end, however, Merton's experience cannot be reduced to a formulaic phrase. What he experienced is essentially ineffable, but we are grateful for his efforts to describe the ineffable.

# Coda

The question we are left with: *Is* Merton still a *wounded* man? It is impossible to know for certain the extent to which Merton was healed of his wounds. Surely, his wounds influenced the person he became; they certainly turned him toward God and likely brought him into the Trappist order. His wounds perhaps effected his becoming a priest and also kept him in the Abbey of Gethsemani.

It is clear, however, to a close reader of his journals, that he indeed became a more *whole* man. Psychological wholeness requires an embracing of our wounds, and Merton finally came to terms with the results of his wounding, for example, recognizing his "refusal of woman," embracing his shadow, to the extent that he could forgive himself for his libertine youth, his exploitation of women, his *comtemptus mundi*, his pride and his willfulness.

At the time of his sudden death, Merton was at the noon-day of his life, his morning soul-searching complete. At the time of his journey to the East, he was at the beginning of the afternoon of his life. Jung says, "We cannot live the afternoon of life according to the programme of life's morning; for what was great in the morning will be little at evening and what in the morning was true will at evening have become a lie. I have given psychological treatment to too many people...not to be moved by this fundamental truth."[1]

There are, consequently, many questions we simply cannot answer. The most often asked question is: "Would Merton have remained a hermit at Gethsemani?" There are many signs indi-

cating that he would have moved on to another hermitage outside of Gethsemani, but to speculate further is an exercise in
futility. What we *do* know is that at the time of his death, Merton
had encountered, while in the presence of the Polonnaruwa
Buddhas, perhaps his most numinous experience here on earth,
and in his last 1968 journal entries he appeared to be a far hap-
pier, far more whole man than the fragmented one who first
entered the Abbey of Gethsemani in 1941.

# Notes

## Introduction

1. Erik Erikson, *Young Man Luther: A Study in Psychoanalysis and History* (New York: W. W. Norton, 1962), 39–40.

2. Thomas Merton, *Turning Toward the World: The Journals of Thomas Merton, Volume Four, 1960–1963* (San Francisco: HarperSanFrancisco, 1997), 323. Hereafter, the Journals—Thomas Merton, *The Journals of Thomas Merton, Volumes 1–7* (San Francisco: HarperSanFrancisco, 1996–99)—will be cited only by volume number.

3. Andrew Samuels, *A Critical Dictionary of Jungian Analysis* (London: Routledge & Kegan Paul, 1986), 160.

4. Thomas Merton, *The Seven Storey Mountain* (New York: Harcourt, Brace & Company, 1948), 372. Hereafter, this will be cited as *SSM*.

## Chapter One

1. William Wordsworth, *Ode: Intimations of Immortality*.

2. *SSM*, 5 (see introduction, n. 4).

3. Ibid., 69.

4. According to a legend, St. Augustine the bishop, while he was thinking about the Holy Trinity, met a child on the beach who was attempting to use a spoon to transfer the waters of the ocean into a small hole. When Augustine explained to him that

this was not possible, the child replied that it was far more foolish to try to find an explanation for the mystery of the Trinity.

5. *SSM*, 16.

6. *Vol. 3*, 337 (see introduction, n. 2).

# Chapter Two

1. *SSM*, 21 (see introduction, n. 4).

2. Ibid., 54.

3. Ibid., 55.

4. Ibid., 61.

5. Ibid., 63.

6. Ibid., 79.

7. Ibid.

8. *Vol. 1*, 452 (see introduction, n. 2).

9. *SSM*, 82.

10. Ibid., 94.

11. Ibid.

12. Andrew Samuels, *A Critical Dictionary of Jungian Analysis* (London: Routledge & Kegan Paul, 1986), 138.

13. *Vol. 4*, 113.

14. *SSM*, 107.

15. Ibid., 109.

16. Ibid., 117.

17. Ibid., 120.

18. Simone Weil, *The Simone Weil Reader: A Legendary Spiritual Odyssey of Our Time*, ed. George A. Panichas (New York: David McKay Company, Inc., 1977), 473.

19. *SSM*, 130–31.

20. Michael Mott, *The Seven Mountains of Thomas Merton* (New York: Harcourt, Brace & Company, 1993), 87.

21. Ibid., 74.

22. *Tricycle: The Buddhist Review*, Summer, 1992: 24.

23. Calvin S. Hall and Verson J. Norby, *A Primer of Jungian Psychology* (New York: A Mentor Book, 1973), 49.

24. *Vol. 5*, 225.

25. *SSM*, 139.

26. Thomas Merton, *In the Dark Before the Dawn: Selected Poems of Thomas Merton*, ed. Lynn R. Szabo (New York: New Directions Book, 2005), 54–55.

27. Monica Furlong, *Merton: A Biography* (San Francisco: Harper & Row Publishers, 1980), 58.

28. Jolande Jacobi, *The Way of Individuation* (New York: A Meridian Book, 1967), 41.

29. *SSM*, 139.

30. Mott, *The Seven Mountains of Thomas Merton*, 78.

31. *SSM*, 147.

32. *Hamlet*, Act I, sc. ii.

33. *The Tempest*, Act 5, sc. i.

# Chapter Three

1. *King Lear*, Act I, sc. iv.

2. *Vol. 6*, 344 (see introduction, n. 2).

3. Carl Jung, *Collected Works of C. G. Jung*, 20 vols., trans. by R. F. C. Hull (Princeton, NJ: Princeton University Press, 1953–79), vol. 9, part 1, 123.

4. *SSM*, 179 (see introduction, n. 4).

5. *Vol. 3*, 20.

6. *SSM*, 182.

7. Thomas Merton, *A Vow of Conversation* (New York: Farrar, Straus & Giroux, 1988), 132.

8. Ibid., 194.

9. *SSM*, 182.

10. Theodore Roethke, *The Collected Poems* (New York: Anchor Books, 1975), 231.

11. T. S. Eliot, *The Complete Poems and Plays, 1909–1950* (New York: Harcourt Brace Jovanovich, Publishers, 1950), 58.

12. C. G. Jung, *Visions Seminars*, vol. 2 (Zurich: Spring Publications, 1976), 409–10.

13. *SSM*, 189.

14. Ibid., 203.

15. St. Augustine, *The Confessions*, trans. by Maria Boulding (Hyde Park, NY: New City Press, 1997), 198.

16. *Vol. 3*, 241.

17. Carl Jung, *Psychological Reflections: A New Anthology of His Writings*, ed. Jolande Jacobi (New York: Bollingen Foundations Inc., 1973), 364.

18. *SSM*, 246.

19. Carl Jung, *Psychology and Western Religion*, trans. by R. F. C. Hull (Princeton: Princeton University Press, 1984), 97.

20. *SSM*, 277.

21. Ibid., 279.

22. Ibid., 284.

23. Ibid., 287.

24. Ibid., 289.

25. Ibid., 326

26. Ibid., 356.

# Chapter Four

1. Karen Horney, *Self-Analysis* (New York: W. W. Norton & Co. 1942), 39–40.

2. *SSM*, 428 (see introduction, n. 4).

3. *Vol. 2*, 316–17 (see introduction, n. 2).

4. Jolande Jacobi, *Way of Individuation* (New York: A Meridian Book, 1967), 109.

5. *Vol. 2*, 319.

6. Ibid., 70.

7. Ibid., 71.

8. Thomas Merton, *Seeds of Contemplation* (New York: A New Directions Book, 1949), 60.

9. *Vol. 2*, 452.

10. Merton, *Seeds*, 50.

11. Thomas Merton, *The Collected Poems of Thomas Merton* (New York: A New Directions Book, 1977), 236.

12. Thomas Merton, *My Argument with the Gestapo* (New York: New Directions Book, 1968), 108.

13. Jacobi, *Way of Individuation*, 47.

14. Thomas Merton, *The Waters of Siloe* (New York: Harcourt and Brace, 1949), 349.

15. Daryl Sharp, *C. G. Jung Lexicon: A Primer of Terms and Concepts* (Toronto: Inner City Books, 1991), 49.

16. Merton, *Seeds*, 22.

17. Ibid., 35.

18. Ibid., 41.

19. *Vol. 2*, 458.

# Chapter Five

1. Monica Furlong, *Merton: A Biography* (San Francisco: Harper & Row Publishers, 1980), 170.

2. *Vol. 2*, 371 (see introduction, n. 2).

3. Ibid., 373.

4. Ibid., 379.

5. Ibid., 38.

6. Ibid., 463.

7. *Vol. 4*, 179.

8. Thomas Merton, *The School of Charity: The Letters of Thomas Merton on Religious Renewal and Spiritual Direction*, ed. By Patrick Hart (New York: Farrar, Straus & Giroux, 1990), 35–36.

9. Ibid., 43.

10. Ibid., 48.

11. Ibid., 53–54.

12. Ibid., 63.

13. Ibid., 75.

14. Ibid., 81.

15. Ibid., 90.

16. Ibid., 95.

17. Ibid., 98.

18. *Notebook Nine, Ad Usum.*

19. C. G. Jung, *Psychology and Western Religion*, trans. R. F. C. Hull, (Princeton: Princeton University Press, 1984), 217.

20. *Vol. 3*, 69.

21. Ibid., 58.

22. Ibid., 59–60.

23. Thomas Merton, *Witness to Freedom: Letters in Times of Crisis*, ed. by William Shannon (New York: Harcourt Brace & Co., 1994), 4.

24. Michael Mott, *The Seven Mountains of Thomas Merton* (New York: Harcourt, Brace & Company, 1993), 297.

25. *Vol. 4*, 302.

26. *Merton Annual*, vol. 4, editors Daggy, Hart, D. Kramer, V. Kramer (New York: AMS Press, 1991), 9.

## Chapter Six

1. John Sanford, *Invisible Partners* (New York: Paulist Press, 1980), 65–66.

2. C. G. Jung, *Memories, Dreams, Reflections* (New York: Random House, 1961), 186.

3. Ibid., 187.

4. *Vol. 3*, 93 (see introduction, n. 2).

5. *Vol. 4*, 176.

6. *Vol. 5*, 259.

7. *Vol. 3*, 176.

8. Jung, source unknown.

9. Thomas Merton, *The Sign of Jonas* (New York: Harcourt, Brace & Company, 1948), 262.

10. Daryl Sharp, *C. G. Jung Lexicon: A Primer of Terms and Concepts*, (Toronto: Inner City Books, 1991), 32.

11. *Vol. 3*, 181.

12. Thomas Merton, *The Courage for Truth: Letters to Writers*, ed. by Christine M. Bochen (New York: Farrar, Straus & Giroux, 1993), 90.

13. Thomas Merton, *Witness to Freedom: Letters in Times of Crisis*, ed. by William Shannon (New York: Harcourt Brace & Co., 1994), 4.

14. *Vol. 4*, 17.

15. *SSM*, 15 (see introduction, n. 4).

16. *Vol. 4*, 17.

17. Ibid., 245–46.

18. Joan Chittister, O.S.B., *The Rule of Benedict: Insights for the Ages* (New York: Crossroad, 2002), 102.

19. *Vol. 5*, 89.

20. Thomas Merton, *The School of Charity: Letters*, ed. by Brother Patrick Hart (New York: Farrar, Straus, Giroux, 1990), 236.

21. Thomas Merton, *A Vow of Conversation* (New York: Farrar, Straus & Giroux, 1988), 101.

22. *Vol. 5*, 167–68.

23. M. L. von France, "The Process of Individuation," in *Man and His Symbols*, ed. by Carl Jung (New York: Dell Publishing Co., 1964), 195.

24. *Vol. 4*, 149.

25. Andrew Samuels, *A Critical Dictionary of Jungian Analysis* (London: Routledge & Kegan Paul, 1986), 135.

26. *Vol. 4*, 149.

27. Michael Mott, *The Seven Mountains of Thomas Merton* (Boston: Houghton Mifflin, 1984), 532.

28. *Vol. 4*, 161–62.

29. *Vol. 5*, 202.

30. Patrick O'Connell, "Sunken Islands: Two and One-Fifth Unpublished Merton Poems," *Merton Seasonal* (Spring 1987): 6.

31. *Vol. 7*, 284.

32. Ibid., 254.

33. Carl Jung, *Man and His Symbols* (New York: Dell Publishing, 1964), 230.

# Chapter Seven

1. William H. Shannon, *Thomas Merton's Dark Path* (New York: Farrar, Straus, Giroux, 1981), 169.

2. Michael Mott, *The Seven Mountains of Thomas Merton*, (New York: Harcourt, Brace & Company, 1993), 292.

3. George Woodcock, *Thomas Merton, Monk and Poet*, (New York: Farrar, Straus, Giroux, 1978), 75, and Mott, *The Seven Mountains*, 293.

4. *Vol. 2*, 463–64 (see introduction, n. 2).

5. *Vol. 4*, 315.

6. Thomas Merton, *Seeds of Contemplation* (New York: A New Directions Book, 1949), 17.

7. Thomas Merton, *Disputed Questions* (New York: Harcourt and Brace, 1985), 189.

8. *Vol. 4*, 87.

9. Merton, *Seeds*, 28.

10. *Vol. 2*, 383.

11. Ibid.

12. Ibid., 462–63.

13. Thomas Merton, *The Collected Poems of Thomas Merton* (New York: A New Directions Book, 1977), 231.

14. Monica Furlong, *Merton: A Biography* (San Francisco: Harper & Row Publishers, 1980), 216.

15. *Vol. 3*, 69.

16. Mott, *Seven Mountains*, 297.

17. *Vol. 3*, 59–60.

18. Mott, *Seven Mountains*, 291.

19. *Vol. 3*, 73.

20. Mott, *Seven Mountains*, 7.

21. Thomas Merton, *Collected Poems*, 238.

22. Furlong, *Merton*, 228.

23. *Vol. 3*, 78.

24. *SSM*, 107 (see introduction, n. 4).

25. *Vol. 3*, 364.

26. Ibid., 57–58.

27. Ibid., 25.

# Chapter Eight

1. *Vol. 3*, 30–32 (see introduction, n. 2).

2. Ibid., 87. Emphasis is in the original.

3. Ibid., 176.

4. Ibid., 182.

5. Ibid., 209.

6. Ibid., 236.

7. Ibid., 294.

8. Ibid., 300.

9. Ibid.

10. Ibid., 307.

11. Ibid., 309.

12. Ibid., 350.

13. Ibid., 346.

14. Ibid., 351.

15. Ibid., 358.

16. *Vol. 4*, 26.

17. Ibid., 53–54.

18. Ibid., 79–80.

19. Thomas Merton, *Witness to Freedom: Letters in Times of Crisis*, ed. By William Shannon (New York: Harcourt, Brace & Co., 1994), 213.

20. *Vol. 4*, 237.

21. Ibid., 253.

22. *Vol. 5*, 278.

23. James Hall, *The Jungian Experience: Analysis and Individuation* (Toronto: Inner City Books, 1986), 44.

24. *Vol. 4*, 323.

25. *Vol. 5*, 22.

26. Ibid., 79.

27. Ibid., 116.

28. Thomas Merton, *Zen and the Birds of Appetite* (New York: A New Directions Book, 1968), 38.

29. *Vol. 5*, 135.

30. Ibid., 154.

31. Ibid., 180.

32. Ibid., 283.

# Chapter Nine

1. *Vol. 5*, 281 (see introduction, n. 2).

2. Thomas Merton, *Witness to Freedom: Letters in Times of Crisis*, ed. William Shannon (New York: Harcourt, Brace & Co., 1994), 4.

3. Thomas Merton, *The Collected Poems of Thomas Merton* (New York: A New Directions Book, 1977), 363.

4. *Vol. 4*, 17.

5. Vol. 2, 392.

6. Merton, *Witness*, 43.

7. Vol. 6, 130–31.

8. Carl Jung, *Man and His Symbols* (New York: Dell Publishing, 1964), 195.

9. Michael Mott, *The Seven Mountains of Thomas Merton* (New York: Harcourt, Brace & Company, 1993), 578.

10. *Vol. 5*, 197–98.

11. *Vol. 6*, 19.

12. Ibid., 23.

13. Ibid., 27.

14. Ibid., 41–42.

15. Jolande Jacobi, *The Way of Individuation* (New York: A Meridian Book, 1967), 45–46.

16. *Vol. 6*, 43–44.

17. Ibid., 45.

18. Ibid.

19. Ibid., 46.

20. Ibid., 47.

21. Ibid., 50.

22. Ibid., 55.

23. Ibid., 66–67.

24. Ibid., 323.

25. Ibid., 77.

26. Ibid., 322.

27. Ibid., 87.

28. Ibid., 328.

29. Ibid.

30. Ibid., 334.

31. Ibid., 327.

32. Ibid., 334.

33. Ibid., 341–42.

34. Ibid., 129.

35. Michael Mott, *The Seven Mountains of Thomas Merton* (New York: Harcourt, Brace & Company, 1993), 457–58.

36. *Vol. 6*, 140.

37. Ibid., 242.

38. Ibid., 241.

39. Ibid., 168–69.

40. *Vol. 7*, 29.

41. Thomas Merton, *The Hidden Ground of Love*, ed. by William Shannon (New York: Farrar, Straus & Giroux, 1985), 501.

42. Ibid., 509.

43. Ibid., 510.

44. *Vol. 6*, 236.

45. Jane Polden, *Regeneration: Journey Through the Mid-Life Crisis* (London: Continuum, 2002), 326.

46. Monica Furlong, *Merton: A Biography* (San Francisco: Harper & Row Publishers, 1980), 337.

47. *Vol. 7*, 157.

# Chapter Ten

1. *Vol. 6*, 297 (see introduction, n. 2).

2. *Vol. 7*, 174.

3. Ibid., 139.

4. Ibid., 332.

5. Ibid., 253.

6. Ibid., 255.

7. Ibid., 266.

8. Ibid.

9. Ibid., 323.

10. Thomas Merton, *Contemplation in a World of Action* (Notre Dame, IN: University of Notre Dame Press, 1998), 206.

11. *Vol. 7*, 323.

12. Simone Weil, *Simone Weil Reader*, ed. by George A. Panichas (New York: McKay Company Inc., 1977), 474.

# Coda

1. Carl Jung, *Modern Man in Search of a Soul* (New York: Harcourt, Brace & World, 1955), 108.

# Glossary

**Anima** (Latin, *soul*). The unconscious, feminine aspect of a man's personality, his inner woman. She is personified in dreams by female figures ranging from harlot to witch to spiritual guide (Sophia). She is the Eros principle; therefore, a man's individuation is reflected in how he relates to people, especially women. Identification with a negative anima appears in a man as moodiness, obstinacy, oversensitivity, and depression.

**Animus** (Latin, *spirit*). The unconscious, masculine aspect of a woman's personality. He personifies the Logos principle. Identification with the animus can cause a woman to be inflexible, opinionated, and disputatious. The animus is a woman's inner man who serves as a bridge between her ego and her own unconscious fecundity.

**Archetypes**. Inherited universal patterns or motifs that abide in the collective unconscious. They serve as the basic foundation and structure of all religion and myth. They cannot be experienced directly, only indirectly through dreams and transcendental experiences.

**Collective Unconscious**. Whereas Freud is credited with the discovery of the personal unconscious (also called subconscious) mind, Jung is credited with the discovery of the collective unconscious (see his autobiography *Memories, Dreams, Reflections*). The collective unconscious is the abode of the archetypes.

**Coniunctio** (Latin, *uniting, joining together*). Jung sees this archetype as the marriage of opposites. A man coming to terms with his anima or a woman coming to terms with her animus experiences the psychic marriage of opposites that in turn results in rebirth and transformation.

**Consciousness**. A person's awareness, intuition, and perception, with a person's function of reflection as its achievement.

**Contemptus Mundi** (Latin, *contempt of the world*). To enter monastic life because one feels that the world is evil is to enter it for the wrong reason. One enters a monastery because one has a special contemplative vocation: to know, love, and serve God.

**Dreams**. "Letters" from the unconscious that reveal the hidden recesses of the psyche, and if reflected upon carefully, they can lead one to greater self-knowledge and wholeness.

**Ego**. The center of consciousness, which in the first part of a person's life is dominant. A person's work in the second part of life is to foster the ego's realization of the Self.

**Eros** (Greek, *love*). The feminine principle of relatedness. In a man it is linked with his anima.

**Ignis Fatuus** (Latin, *foolish fire*). Will-o'-the-wisp, delusive hope. Jung considers a person's search for perfection as a delusion; in a lifetime a person can only hope to achieve wholeness.

**Individuation**. The process of the conscious realization of psychic reality. Its ultimate goal is the awareness of the Self.

**Inflation**. Too high or too low an opinion of one's self. Its antidote is self-knowledge.

**Libido**. Refers to energy. Freud sees libido as connected to sexuality. Jung sees it in a more general fashion. In short, it is psychic energy, not only sexual energy. When a person is cured of neurosis, the individual experiences a flow of energy, libido.

**Locus Dei** (Latin, *place of God*). God is omnipresent, present not only in churches and monasteries but also within our souls.

**Logos** (Greek, *word*). The masculine principle of discrimination. In a woman it is linked with her animus.

**Mandala**. From the Sanskrit word meaning "magic circle." It can be a geometric figure of a squared or circled square. It is a symbol of the Self; therefore, it is a symbol of wholeness.

**Persona**. (Latin, *actor's mask*) The face (mask) we present to the world. The danger is that overidentification with the persona hinders self-knowledge since the persona represents only our social role in life.

**Projection**. The process by which an unconscious quality or trait is cast onto others (including collective things like races and countries and cities). Projection of the anima or animus onto a real woman or man is the dynamic of falling in love. The danger is that we make people in our own image, instead of seeing them as they truly are.

**Quaternity**. A fourfold image, usually square or circular and symmetrical. It is the symbol of wholeness.

**Self**. The archetype of wholeness, which is also the regulating center of the personality. For Western man the Self is Christ.

**Shadow**. Unconscious characteristics or traits of the personality that the ego tends to reject, deny, or ignore. It is personified in dreams by figures of the same sex as the dreamer. Consciously integrating the shadow into our life is one of the main tasks of individuation, a task that leads to an increase of energy.

**Synchronicity**. A causal connecting principle. Jung describes synchronicity as a "meaningful coincidence" between the outer world and the inner world.

**Unconscious**. Jung sees the unconscious as that portion of the psyche that is not available to the conscious mind. It is everything that is not known or available to the ego, the center of consciousness.

**Wholeness**. The mature and full expression of all aspects of one's personality. It is connected not only with one's self but also with other people and the environment. It is also derived from the same word for "holiness": It is the purpose of life, echoing Christ's injunction, "Be ye whole as your heavenly Father is whole." The latter is how Jung would translate Christ's dictum, because he believed the Greek word for "perfect" was closer in meaning to the word whole. Wholeness is possible for people, perfection an *ignis fatuus*.

# Bibliography

## Paperback versions of Thomas Merton's Journals

Merton, Thomas. *Run to the Mountain: The Journals of Thomas Merton, Volume One, 1939–1941*. Edited by Patrick Hart, OCSO. San Francisco: HarperSanFranciso, 1996.

———. *Entering the Silence: The Journals of Thomas Merton, Volume Two, 1941–1952*. Edited by Jonathan Montaldo. San Francisco: HarperSanFrancisco, 1997.

———. *A Search for Solitude: The Journals of Thomas Merton, Volume Three, 1952–1960*. Edited by Lawrence S. Cunningham. San Francisco: HarperSanFrancisco, 1997.

———. *Turning Toward the World: The Journals of Thomas Merton, Volume Four, 1960–1963*. Edited by Victor A. Kramer. San Francisco: HarperSanFrancisco, 1997.

———. *Dancing in the Water of Life: The Journals of Thomas Merton, Volume Five, 1963–1965*. Edited by Robert E. Daggy. San Francisco: HarperSanFrancisco, 1997.

———. *Learning to Love: The Journals of Thomas Merton, Volume Six, 1966–1967*. Edited by Christine M. Bochen. San Francisco: HarperSanFrancisco, 1998.

———. *The Other Side of the Mountain: The Journals of Thomas Merton, Volume Seven, 1967–1968*. Edited by Patrick Hart, OCSO. San Francisco: HarperSanFrancisco, 1999.

# Continued Bibliography

Furlong, Monica. *Merton: A Biography*, San Francisco: Harper & Row Publishers, 1980.

Horney, Karen. *Self-Analysis*. New York: W. W. Norton & Co. 1942.

Jacobi, Jolande. *The Way of Individuation*. New York: A Meridian Book, 1967.

Jung, C. G. *Man and His Symbols*. New York: Dell Publishing, 1964.

Jung, C. G. *Memories, Dreams, Reflections*. New York: Random House, 1961.

Jung, C. G. *Modern Man in Search of a Soul*. New York: Harcourt, Brace & World, 1955.

Jung, C. G. *Psychological Reflections: A New Anthology of His Writings*. Edited by Jolande Jacobi. New York: Bollingen Foundations Inc., 1973.

Jung, C. G. *Psychology and Western Religion*. Translated by R. F. C. Hull. Princeton: Princeton University Press, 1984.

Merton, Thomas. *The Collected Poems of Thomas Merton*. New York: A New Directions Book, 1977.

Merton, Thomas. *Contemplation in a World of Action*. Notre Dame, IN: University of Notre Dame Press, 1998.

Merton, Thomas. *The Courage for Truth: Letters to Writers*. New York: Farrar, Straus and Giroux, 1993.

Merton, Thomas. *Disputed Questions*. New York: Harcourt and Brace, 1985.

Merton, Thomas. *In the Dark Before the Dawn: Selected Poems of Thomas Merton*. Edited by Lynn R. Szabo. New York: New Directions Book, 2005.

Merton, Thomas. *My Argument with the Gestapo*. New York: New Directions Book, 1968.

Merton, Thomas. *New Seeds of Contemplation*. New York: New Directions Press, 1961.

Merton, Thomas. *The School of Charity: Letters*. Edited by Brother Patrick Hart. New York: Farrar, Straus, Giroux, 1990.

Merton, Thomas. *Seeds of Contemplation*. New York: New Directions Press, 1949.

Merton, Thomas. *The Seven Storey Mountain*. New York: Harcourt, Brace & Company, 1948.

Merton, Thomas. *The Sign of Jonas*. New York: Harcourt, Brace & Company, 1953.

Merton, Thomas. *A Vow of Conversation*. New York: Farrar, Straus & Giroux, 1988.

Merton, Thomas. *The Waters of Siloe*. New York: Harcourt and Brace, 1949.

Merton, Thomas. *Witness to Freedom: Letters in Times of Crisis*. Edited by William Shannon. New York: Harcourt Brace & Co., 1994.

Merton, Thomas. *Zen and the Birds of Appetite*. New York: A New Directions Book, 1968.

Mott, Michael. *The Seven Mountains of Thomas Merton*. New York: Harcourt, Brace & Company, 1993.

Polden, Jane. *Regeneration: Journey Through the Mid-Life Crisis*. London: Continuum, 2002.

Samuels, Andrew. *A Critical Dictionary of Jungian Analysis*. London: Routledge & Kegan Paul, 1986.

Shannon, William H. *Thomas Merton's Dark Path*. New York: Farrar, Straus, Giroux, 1981.

Sharp, Daryl. *C. G. Jung Lexicon: A Primer of Terms and Concepts*. (Toronto: Inner City Books, 1991.

Weil, Simone. *Simone Weil Reader*. Edited by George A. Panichas. New York: McKay Company, Inc., 1977.

Woodcock, George. *Thomas Merton, Monk and Poet*. New York: Farrar, Straus, Giroux, 1978.

## Other Books by Robert Waldron
## Published by Paulist Press

Thomas Merton: Master of Attention

Walking with Gerard Manley Hopkins

Walking with Henri Nouwen

Walking with Kathleen Norris

Walking with Thomas Merton